3

GREAT PRESERVED LOCOMOTIVES

'PRINCESS ROYAL' No 6201
PRINCESS ELIZABETH

Edited on behalf of
The Princess Elizabeth Locomotive Society Ltd
by
Clive Mojonnier

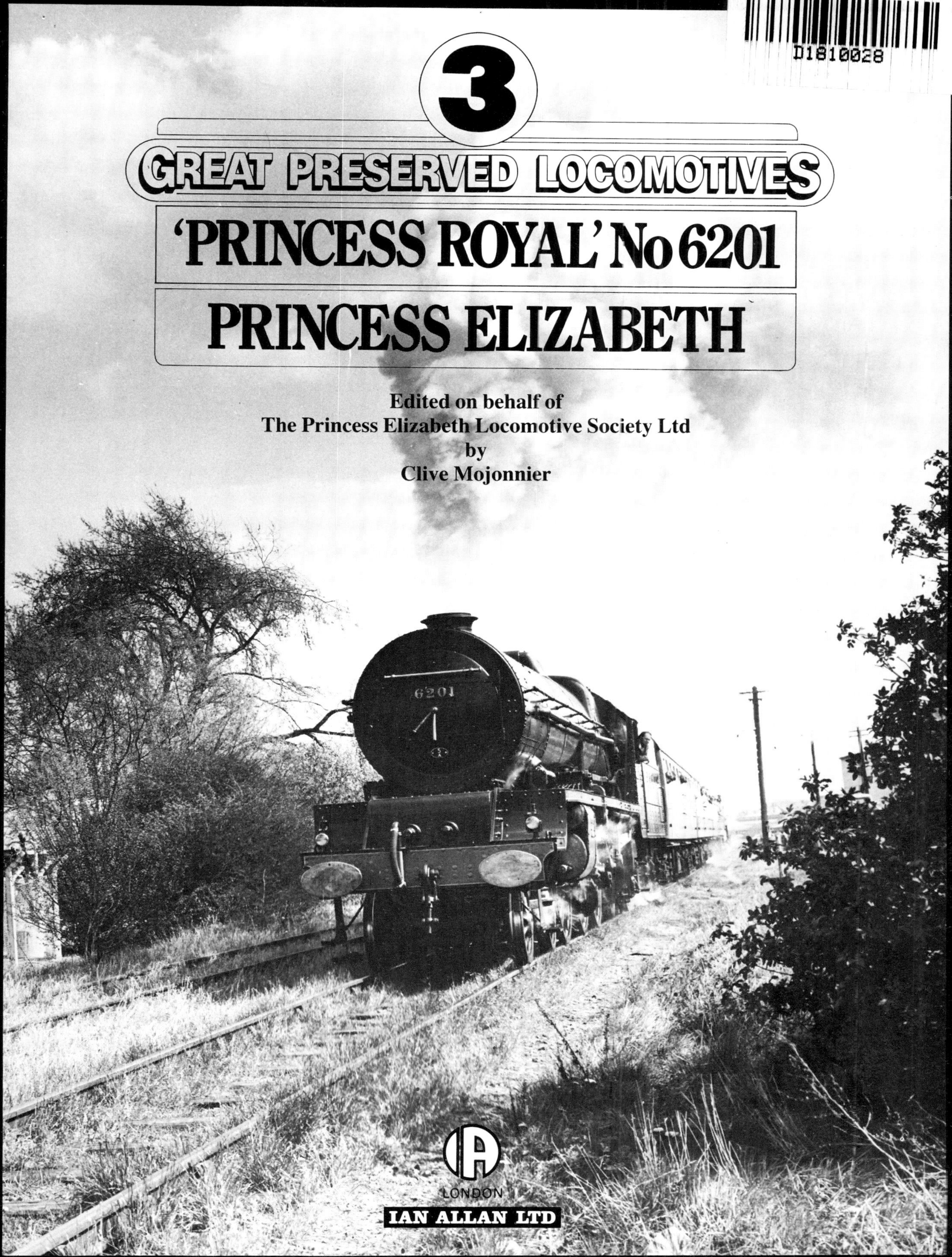

LONDON
IAN ALLAN LTD

Contents

First published 1985

ISBN 0 7110 1537 6

Published by Ian Allan Ltd, Shepperton, Surrey;
and printed by Ian Allan Printing Ltd at their works
at Coombelands in Runnymede, England

Preface

The history of a locomotive such as No 6201
can never be complete, but this book is an
attempt to trace some part of it.

Through the years the society has seen
many changes. The initial fund was to save
the locomotive for static display, but without
the three-man partnership formed in 1961 no
history would have been possible. No 6201 as
well as being a record holder, represented the
pride of our largest railway company and the
people who served it in the 1930s. Because of
the efforts made in 1961, No 6201 has been
given a second chance on main line duties,
albeit for pleasure. It is to be hoped that
some of the hard work connected with
keeping a locomotive up to main line running
standards, is conveyed in the following pages.

We rely on our members to support us
through the good and bad periods, but also
to other friends who contribute in various
ways. Without members, we cannot continue
to preserve a world record holder for a future
generation.

Sincere thanks are due to the following,
who have been of great assistance in the
preparation of this book: Messrs Ian Allan
Ltd, G. Allen, K. Andrews, Mrs N.
Blackhurst, D. Fleet, W. Hudson, A. Shaw,
Mrs. C. Windsor, Miss J. Wilcox.

My wife, whose understanding and
patience have been tested to the full, earns
my heartfelt thanks.

The author is always grateful for any
further historical or interesting facts, which
may come to light with regard to No 6201's
work between 1933–1962. Any such
information can be sent to me directly or via
the publishers.

Clive Mojonnier,
London E4 8BD.

January 1985

Cover:
**No 6201 leaves Hereford with the 'Western
Jubilee' on 1 October 1977.** *J. H. Cooper-Smith*

Previous page:
**No 6201 at its home base, the Bulmer Railway
Centre, Hereford.** *6201 Society*

Right:
***Princess Elizabeth* 6201 at Shrewsbury station
with an 85C shed plate fitted. An
acknowledgement for the efforts put in by
the Hereford crews on her second main line
career.** *Peter J.C. Skelton*

Below:
**Un-named and fitted with shelter for
indicating tests shortly after construction in
November 1933.** *W.H. Whitworth*

Introduction

The late Derek Cross had expressed a wish to ride on No 6201's footplate. Sadly this was not to be fulfilled. Therefore, the following introduction sums up what I feel is not only relevant to Stanier Pacifics, but is a small tribute to his work over many years.

What is one's immediate reaction to the sight of some great mountain, an Everest or an Eiger, emerging from the morning mists? Is it a mental calculation of the rocks or of the titanic forces that went into the making of so massive a structure? Or is it simply a sense of awe that one small planet could have produced such a splendid vision? To me, at any rate, the same mental conflict occurred every time I saw one of Stanier's mighty Pacifics. What was the more impressive, the engineering that went into the machines' make-up, or the fact that so large and splendid a locomotive could have been built within the limits of the puny British loading gauge? My simile is apt for the Stanier Pacifics were giants among British locomotives and in my mind will always be engines of the hills. The rolling Midlands or the grime of Merseyside seemed to have no part in the life of these machines although much of their work was done in such surroundings. Instead, the two great banks of Beattock and Shap, or the lesser climbs through the Nith Valley and up the valley of the Allan Water epitomised their true environment. Throughout the history of the LNW, the Caledonian, the LMS, and in the steam era on BR, these climbs were the yardstick by which West Coast locomotive performance was judged. They were the pit into which the Midlandisation of the infant LMS stumbled, and which some 30 years later came to be the albatross around the necks of the 'Britannias' in the last twilight hours of steam. If these great northern banks were ever tamed by steam it was by the Stanier Pacifics, though I have known even 'Duchesses' in trouble after a check on a misty morning at Shap Wells, or a 'Lizzie' very glad to see Beattock summit on an evening of storm.

So much has been written about the inception of the Stanier Pacifics that I am not going to retread old ground. Suffice it to say that by the early 1930s the need of the LMS for a large and powerful Pacific was overwhelming. Such ideas had been kicked around in drawing offices at Derby and Crewe since the formation of the LMS in

1923 but in every case had perished on the rock of objections to axle loading by the civil engineers, to whom light axleloads were like the Holy Grail – regardless of how these loads were distributed or how forces such as hammer blow were dispersed. In retrospect, locomotive engineering on Britain's railways has been far more hampered by the false fears of the civil engineers than by loading gauge restrictions. In all fairness, in the early days of railways the civil engineers had nothing to go by, but the tragedy was that having nothing they kept it far too long. Stanier's first two Pacifics Nos 6200/1 were very much based on the Churchward precepts as developed to their final form at that time in the GWR 'Kings'. Much has been written about minor faults in these two engines as

first produced; the boiler barrels were too long, the superheat was too low and the Midland pattern tender was too small – both

TECHNICAL DATA

	No 6200 as built	Nos 6200–1 and 6203–12 as modified
Cylinders (4), diameter:	16¼in	16¼in
Cylinders (4), stroke:	28in	28in
Driving wheels, diameter:	6ft 6in	6ft 6in
Bogie wheels diameter:	3ft 0in	3ft 0in
Trailing wheels diameter:	3ft 9in	3ft 9in
Wheelbase, coupled:	15ft 3in	15ft 3in
Wheelbase, total engine:	37ft 9in	37ft 9in
Heating surface, firebox:	190sq ft	217sq ft
Heating surface, tubes and flues:	2,523sq ft	2,299sq ft
Heating surface, total:	2,713sq ft	2,516sq ft
Superheating surface:	370sq ft	598sq ft
Firegrate area:	45sq ft	45sq ft
Working pressure, per sq in:	250lb	250lb
Adhesion weight:	67·5 tons	67·5 tons
Weight of engine in working order:	104·5 tons	104·5 tons
Water capacity of tender:	4,000gal	4,000gal
Coal capacity of tender:	9ton	10ton
Weight of engine and tender:	158·6ton	160·1ton
Maximum height above rail:	13ft 2in	13ft 2in
Maximum width:	9ft 0in	9ft 0in
Engine and tender, length overall:	74ft 4¼in	74ft 4¼in
Tractive effort (at 85% b.p.):	40,300lb	40,300lb

Note: No 6202 (turbine driven) had boiler generally uniform with Nos 6203–12. Weight of No 6202 in working order, 110·6 tons; adhesion weight, 69 tons.

Above right:
No 6201 with Stanier 10 ton tender, attached after the record run of 1936, this being the same tender which No 6201 hauls today. *LPC/Real Photos (47505)*

Below right:
No 46201 at Shap Wells 29 July 1960.
The late Derek Cross

Below:
No 6201 as built with 9 ton Fowler tender in 1933, and domeless boiler.
LPC/Real Photos (47551)

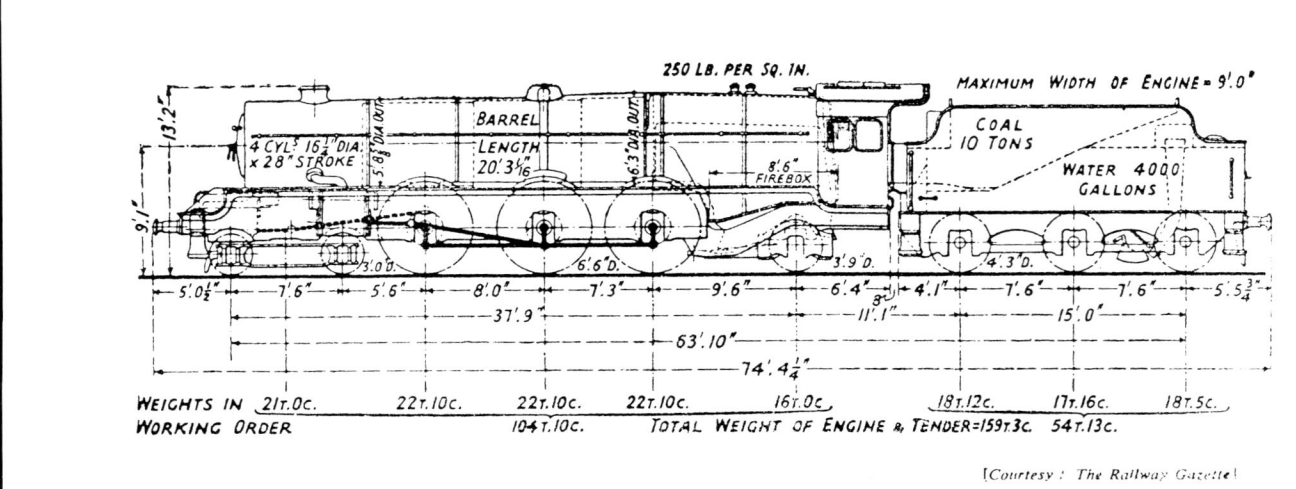

250 LB. PER SQ. IN.   MAXIMUM WIDTH OF ENGINE = 9'.0"

[Courtesy : The Railway Gazette]

practically and aesthetically. What is amazing is not what was wrong but how much was right. Another factor that cannot be stressed enough is that these engines were built from scratch in 18 months. This says a lot for their design and designer, but also speaks wonders for the versatility and vitality of Crewe Works. Whatever may be written about Webb, had he never designed a successful engine (and he designed many) his name would still stand by his layout and development of Crewe and its traditions.

If the entry into service of most of the 'Duchess' class passed relatively unnoticed on account of wartime conditions, the manner of their going is one of the saddest and most surprising in British railway history. By 1960, and with BR set on a long term programme of dieselisation, it was inevitable that sooner, or later, the days of the Stanier Pacifics were numbered. It was also logical that the older and less powerful 'Princesses' would be the first to go, and, indeed, the first four (Nos 46204/10–12) were withdrawn in the week ending 7 October 1961. The remainder of the class followed in the next 12 months, but not before Upperby and Kingmoor's trio, Nos 46200/1/3, had staged a brilliant Indian summer on the Perth expresses, as well as standing in for Class 40s whose record for reliability at this time was less than startling.

What is certain is that by 1964 the LMR had too many large engines for reasons that I have not space to go into in detail. What is also certain is that the Stanier Pacifics were cut down in their prime without any blemish of their design or mechanical ability. To many of us who knew these mighty engines the end of steam came not on 11 August 1968, but on 12 September 1964. The trout had gone, the tiddlers remained. As Shakespeare said of Caesar 'Why man, he doth bestride the narrow world like a Colossus'. There could be no better epitaph for Stanier's Pacifics.

Right:
The elegant lines of No 46201 *Princess Elizabeth* are shown in this photograph in green livery as she tops Beattock summit in August 1962 with the morning Euston–Perth express which at this time carried a through portion to Aberdeen. *The late Derek Cross*

Summary of Numbers, Names, Dates and Allocations
'Princess Royal' class and Turbine locomotive

LMS No	BR No	Name	Date Built	Date Withdrawn	Shed Allocation 9/50	Shed Allocation 10/57	Final Shed	Notes
6200	46200	*Princess Royal*	6/33	11/62	Edge Hill	Edge Hill	Carlisle Kingmoor	
6201	46201	*Princess Elizabeth*	11/33	10/62	Edge Hill	Crewe North	Carlisle Upperby	1
6202	46202	*Princess Anne*	6/35	5/54	Camden	—	Camden	2
6203	46203	*Princess Margaret Rose*	7/35	10/62	Edge Hill	Crewe North	Carlisle Kingmoor	3
6204	46204	*Princess Louise*	7/35	10/61	Edge Hill	Edge Hill	Edge Hill	
6205	46205	*Princess Victoria*	7/35	11/61	Edge Hill	Crewe North	Willesden	
6206	46206	*Princess Marie Louise*	8/35	11/62	Crewe North	Crewe North	Camden	
6207	46207	*Princess Arthur of Connaught*	8/35	11/61	Crewe North	Edge Hill	Willesden	
6208	46208	*Princess Helena Victoria*	8/35	10/62	Crewe North	Edge Hill	Edge Hill	
6209	46209	*Princess Beatrice*	8/35	9/62	Crewe North	Crewe North	Camden	
6210	46210	*Lady Patricia*	9/35	10/61	Crewe North	Edge Hill	Carlisle Kingmoor	
6211	46211	*Queen Maud*	9/35	11/61	Crewe North	Crewe North	Crewe North	
6212	46212	*Duchess of Kent*	10/35	10/61	Crewe North	Crewe North	Crewe North	

Building details
All locomotives built at Crewe. Lot Numbers, 6200/1 Lot 99, 6202 Lot 100, 6203-12 Lot 120.

Notes
1) Preserved in working order by Princess Elizabeth Locomotive Society, Bulmer Railway Centre, Hereford.
2) Popularly known as the Turbomotive, this locomotive was powered by a Metropolitan–Vickers steam turbine. It was rebuilt as a conventional engine in August 1952 and was named at the same time. It was damaged beyond economic repair in the Harrow disaster of October 1952 but was not officially withdrawn until May 1954.
3) Originally on static display at Butlin's Pwllheli Holiday Camp and now at the Midland Railway Trust at Butterley.

SIR WILLIAM STANIER

by W. B. Hudson

The first railway journey I can remember was from Cambridge to Eskmeals on the Furness line. At Cambridge the carriages must have been just out of the paint shop and they gleamed in their livery of 'plum and spilt milk'. (Yes, it really was the London & North Western.) I can also recollect the express for the north running into Bletchley with a big black engine at its head. It was probably a 'Precursor' or 'George V' class, although I did not know it at the time.

Later I lived in Kent but made numerous journeys to the Midlands. After the South Eastern & Chatham, the West Coast main line seemed a magnificent railway, with its mass of flying and burrowing junctions between Euston and Camden, its tall signals, the deep cuttings at Tring and the long Kilsby Tunnel with its wide ventilating shafts. The trains ran smoothly on the 60ft rails, the longest used on any British railway

at that time, and this gave them a very distinctive sound. As far as I can remember, the Birmingham two-hour expresses kept good time. We always travelled LMS and I knew nothing of 'God's Wonderful Railway', which provided a similar two-hour service over its shorter but more steeply-graded route between the two cities.

At other times we went to Lichfield and I spent hours hanging over the fence at Trent Valley. During my early visits the principal trains were handled by 'Royal Scots', with 'Claughtons' and many smaller L&NW types helping out. Then in 1931 I saw a paragraph in the *Meccano Magazine* which gave me some disturbing news. William Stanier from Swindon had been appointed Chief Mechanical Engineer of the LMS and I visualised the graceful L&NW and Midlands engines giving way to taper-boilered monstrosities. On my next visit to Lichfield I

saw *Princess Elizabeth* and *The Princess Royal* working the London to Glasgow expresses and realised that my worst fears had been groundless. The new Pacifics, despite their tapered boilers, were handsome machines (No 6201 was described as the most elegant engine in the Shildon cavalcade by an eminent photographer) and they proved more than capable of carrying out the tasks assigned to them.

Below:
First view of W.A. Stanier's 'Princess Royal' No 6200 at Euston with Fowler tender, on 28 June 1933 without nameplates. The original caption made much of the utmost secrecy about its construction at Crewe works.
BBC Hulton Picture Library

William Arthur Stanier came from a family with a railway background. His father, W.H. Stanier, had been confidential clerk to Dean and was, in fact, his right-hand man. The young Stanier, born in 1876, entered the railway service at the first opportunity and became an apprentice on 27 May 1892, his 16th birthday. The first engine he worked on was a Dean 4-4-0, and he helped with the task of changing many of this engineer's 2-2-0s to 4-2-0s.

It was the practice at Swindon to move those marked for promotion from one section to another and so give them an all-round experience. In 1897, when Stanier had completed his apprenticeship, he went to the drawing office. This appointment came at a vital time, for the methods of Dean were giving way to the ideas of Churchward. The first of the new domeless boilers was being produced. The graceful Dean engines were being superseded by the new products with tapered boilers and high Belpaire fireboxes. These externally ugly machines were, at first, called some rude names, but the running-shed staff soon found out that the new machines were of sound design, and this was especially true of the boilers, which gave long, trouble-free service and low maintenance costs.

In 1900, Stanier left the drawing office and became Inspector of Materials. He played a leading role in developing new methods, but one year later he was transferred to the running side and became Technical Inspector for the Divisional Carriage & Wagon Superintendent at Swindon. Thus he was in the right spot to assist in the testing of the new locomotives and to observe their performance on the road.

In 1903, Stanier was sent, as a temporary measure, to take charge at Westbourne Park during the absence of John Armstrong, who was away on a visit to America for several

months. Stanier went back to Swindon in October of that year, but in 1904 he was again transferred to London as assistant to Armstrong. He went back to Swindon once more in 1906 as assistant to the Works Manager, and later in that year he became Divisional Locomotive Superintendent. This was not an important post in itself, but as the running shed was opposite to the locomotive works, all trials and running-in turns of engines built, modified or repaired, were entrusted to the Swindon shed. So once again he was on the spot when Churchward's new engines were entering service. He became even more involved in the design and construction of these engines when in 1912 he was appointed Assistant Locomotive Works Manager. By this time C.B. Collett had been made assistant to the Chief Mechanical Engineer and the partnership of Collett and Stanier was to last for 19 years.

During World War 1 the works at Swindon produced many guns and other munitions. After the war the Great Western made tremendous efforts to get back as quickly as possible to prewar standards. Churchward retired at the end of 1921 and Collett became Chief Mechanical Engineer. A little earlier, in 1920, Stanier had been promoted to the position of Works Manager. The amalgamation of 1923 made little difference to the GWR, for all it meant was that a few Welsh railways were absorbed and the company was spared the trouble that reorganisation brought to other railways.

The 'Castle' class was introduced in 1923 and, in the locomotive exchange of 1925, proved more than a match for the imposing Pacifics which Gresley had designed for the London & North Eastern Railway. In 1927 the first of the 'King' class was completed, and within a few weeks was shipped to the USA to take part in the centenary celebrations of the Baltimore & Ohio

Railroad. The Americans were much impressed by the fine workmanship and the precision of the construction. Stanier accompanied the engine and his presence doubtless added much to the smooth way in which all the events of the visit took place.

With the introduction of the 'King' class, the peak of locomotive development had been reached at Swindon. New engines continued to be built, but they were of existing classes or modifications of older designs. We must, therefore, move to the

"Princess Royal" Class
4-6-2   **7P**

Designed : Stanier, 1933-5, L.M.S.
Driving Wheels : 6′ 6″.
Cyls. (4) : 16¼″ × 28″.
Tractive Effort : 40,300 lb.
Superheated. Walschaerts Valve Gear

6200	The Princess Royal
6201	Princess Elizabeth
6202	*
6203	Princess Margaret Rose
6204	Princess Louise
6205	Princess Victoria
6206	Princess Marie Louise
6207	Princess Arthur of Connaught
6208	Princess Helena Victoria
6209	Princess Beatrice
6210	Lady Patricia
6211	Queen Maud
6212	Duchess of Kent

Total 13

N.B.—6200 and 6201 built 1933, the rest 1935.
*Turbine driven locomotive.

As the class appeared in the Ian Allan *abc of LMS Locomotives 1945*

London, Midland & Scottish Railway and see what was happening there. The two main constituents of the LMS were the London & North Western and the Midland. Both of these had been fine railways in their heyday (the L&NW was the self-styled 'Premier Line'), but they differed greatly in their operating methods. The Midland believed in a service of frequent but light trains hauled by comparatively small engines which they were said to treat like pets. On the other hand, expresses on the L&NW main line were heavily loaded and engines were thrashed along, often with the pattering of cinders on the carriage roofs as an accompaniment. It so happened that at the time of the amalgamation many senior officials of the L&NW had recently retired or were close to retiring age and, as a consequence, most of the senior posts on the LMS went to ex-Midland officials. The attempt by them to introduce the Midland small-engine policy on the West Coast main line met with considerable opposition from Crewe and the North Western men. This was especially so in the case of the 'Compounds', which were built in considerable numbers. Memories of the unreliability of the Webb compounds caused distrust of further locomotives involving the compound system.

It was soon realised, however, that something more powerful was needed and Sir Henry Fowler, a former Midland man who had taken over as Chief Mechanical Engineer after the brief reign of Hughes, prepared designs for a compound Pacific and the project proceeded far enough for some components to be manufactured. Suddenly Fowler was the victim of what must be the greatest slight ever handed out by a major railway company to its Chief Mechanical Engineer. By whom and how the decision was made seems shrouded in mystery, the GWR 'Castle' proved to be more than master of its job and Fowler was ordered to scrap plans for his compound Pacific to approach the Great Western for a set of plans for a 'Castle' and to put in hand the construction of some 'Improved Castles' for the LMS. The Great Western was always secretive about the doings of its Locomotive Department and refused to lend the plans. The Southern Railway was more helpful, however, and supplied a set of drawings of their new 'Lord Nelson' class engine.

With help from the design department of the North British Locomotive Company, a large three-cylinder 4-6-0 was planned and 50 examples of what was to become known as the 'Royal Scot' class were ordered straight off the drawing board. To build such a large number of engines in such a rush, and ones of mixed parentage at that, was asking for trouble. To everyone's surprise, however, the 'Royal Scots' turned out to be good engines, having considerably more power than the 'Claughtons' and being much more economical in their coal consumption. However, after a time the coal consumption increased alarmingly, but this was traced to the leakage of steam past the single Schmidt wide-piston ring and the economical running returned when this component was replaced by a number of narrower rings.

By now, the dynamic Sir Josiah Stamp was Chairman of the company, and in 1930 Sir Henry Fowler was 'kicked upstairs' to the post of Vice-President and E.J.H. Lemon was appointed Chief Mechanical Engineer. As he was a carriage & wagon man it was obvious that this appointment was of an interim nature, done to give the executive time to look round for a new man. To have appointed someone from Derby or Crewe would simply have renewed the old conflict. It had to be someone from outside, and what was more natural than that the man should be from Swindon, with that works' reputation for sound design and fine engineering.

Thus it came about that Stanier was asked out to lunch by Lemon and during the meal they were joined by Sir Harold Hartley a vice-president of the LMS. Soon another invitation to lunch came from Sir Harold, and this time the suggestion was put forward that Stanier should consider transferring to the LMS. Stanier was embarrassed by this and reported the matter to Collett, who passed the information on to the General Manager of the GWR. The Great Western Chairman joined in the discussion and

pointed out that if Stanier waited for Collett's retirement to step in to the position of CME of the GWR he would have but a few years before his own retirement. A few days later an official approach was made to the Great Western and arrangements were put in hand which resulted in W.A. Stanier becoming Chief Mechanical Engineer of the LMS on 1 January 1932.

On the LMS his job was to build a range of standard locomotives which would be able to cover the complete traction requirements of the system, but the classes of engine should be restricted to the least number which would meet these requirements. This

Above:
The third 'Princess Royal' Pacific was turned out in 1935 as the unique Stanier/ Metropolitan–Vickers steam turbine locomotive. 'Turbomotive' as it became known is seen at Shrewsbury. *Real Photos (R7401)*

Below:
The other side of No 6202 as seen on the Camden turntable. *Real Photos (7231)*

was to be done by building locomotives which would have greater availability because they would need a reduced amount of repairing and servicing. Engines constructed would also be more economical because they would be masters of the work allocated them and consequently would be capable of achieving greater daily mileages.

Stanier believed in team work and he was always generous in acknowledging the work of his staff. There must have been many who did not approve of his appointment, others whose practices were ones with which he disagreed, and yet again officials in high places who did not measure up to the standards he required. It would have been easy to have provoked antagonism by making wholesale changes. But Stanier was a tactful man and a good leader and one of his qualities was that he was able to get the best out of his colleagues. By the use of discreet methods he gradually assembled a group of men of high ability and welded them into a team. The fact that many of these men rose to high positions in later days proved how good he was in picking the right assistants.

The appearance of the first new designs was eagerly awaited, but of course they did not come at once. Some 0-4-4 tanks and some more locomotives of the 'Patriot' class (known as 'Baby Scots' in their early days because in appearance they looked like smaller versions of the 'Royal Scot' class) were the first to appear, but of course their construction had been started before Stanier took office.

The first actual Stanier design to appear was a 2-6-0 similar in size and power to the Horwich-built 'Crabs', but without the steeply inclined cylinders of these engines. The boiler was domeless and the first locomotive had a GWR type 'coffee pot' cover over the safety valves, which were centrally situated on the boiler. Stanier was displeased with this, however, and made it clear that he did not want his engines to look like copies of Swindon products. The appendage was hurriedly removed before the engine appeared on public view. In its place a different shape of cover was provided which gave the engine the appearance of having a small dome. Later engines had the safety valves placed on the top of the firebox.

It was soon rumoured, however, that a Pacific was under construction at Crewe, and when No 6200 The Princess Royal appeared in August 1933 it was seen to have the same basic dimensions as a Great Western 'King'. Wheels 6ft 6in in diameter, boiler pressure of 250lb/sq in and cylinders 16¼in by 28in gave the same tractive effort of 40,300lb at 85% boiler working pressure, but the LMS engine had the advantage of a much larger boiler and firebox. Great Western features incorporated in the locomotive included a tapered domeless boiler and a long piston stroke. There were also many differences, one of the most important being that four sets of Walschaerts valve motion were provided instead of two sets, with rocking levers operating the valves for the other two cylinders. One feature which caused doubt was the retention of the Churchward tradition of providing only a moderate

amount of superheat. Swindon engines were used to using best quality Welsh coal. On the LMS, however, 'Yorkshire Hards' or soft Scottish coals were provided, and with these coals boiler pressure could not always be maintained. This meant that steam entering the cylinders was often at a lower temperature than it should have been. This inadequate provision was soon noted, however, and when 10 further engines were built in 1935, the number of superheater elements was increased from 16 to 32.

Stanier went on to design many more fine engines for the LMS. The 4-6-0 mixed traffic engines known as 'Black Fives' must have been one of the finest investments in revenue earning capacity ever made by a British railway, and 842 of them were eventually built. His 'Jubilee' 4-6-0 express engines introduced in 1934 were, at first, one of his few failures and proved much inferior to the parallel-boiler 'Patriots' on which they were intended to be an improvement. The engines did not steam well, but one of the strong points about Stanier was that once he realised that a mistake had been made he was the first to admit it and lost no time in putting it right. Modifications to the boiler proportions were made and these engines eventually became capable performers. Another important design was his Class 8 2-8-0, of which 852 were ultimately constructed. Many of these engines went overseas to help with the war effort, where they served in many theatres of conflict, but not all returned to the LMS or its successor.

When it was decided to run a high-speed service from London to Glasgow, called the 'Coronation Scot', a further development of the Pacifics took place. In 1937, No 6220 Coronation emerged from Crewe Works. A 40-element superheater was used, driving wheels were increased to 6ft 9in in diameter, and heating surface went up from 2,967sq ft to 3,637sq ft. Coronation carried a streamlined casing, but some later locomotives of this class were built without this feature. These engines at first were known by the clumsy title of the 'Princess Coronation' class, but later they became generally termed 'Duchesses'. They eventually numbered 38.

Another important development made by Stanier was the rebuilding of the experimental high-pressure locomotive No 6399 Fury into what was virtually a tapered-boiler 'Royal Scot'. It proved itself to be superior to the original 'Royal Scots' and eventually the whole 'Royal Scot' class was rebuilt with tapered boilers and with other improvements.

The outbreak of war in 1939 brought a halt, for the time being, to further locomotive development, otherwise we might have seen a super 'Duchess' with a 4-8-2 wheel arrangement.

In the summer of 1942 Stanier was seconded to the Ministry of Production to form one of a team of three full-time scientific advisers. He continued nominally to be CME of the LMS, but his actual absence brought changes to the department. C.E. Fairburn, who had been appointed in 1937 to a post combining the duties of

Electrical Engineer and Deputy Chief Mechanical Engineer, took over as acting CME, but, as he was mainly concerned with electrical engineering, responsibility for steam locomotive matters rested on the shoulders of his principal assistant H.G. Ivatt (son of H.A. Ivatt, famous CME of the Great Northern Railway).

In 1943, Stanier was in the New Year's Honour's List. For his distinguished services to locomotive engineering, and to mechanical engineering practice in general, he was awarded a Knighthood which he received from King George VI at Buckingham Palace on 9 February 1943. The same Honours List included the name of R.A. Riddles, who had held the post of Mechanical & Electrical Engineer, Scotland, since 1937, but who had been seconded to the Government as Director of Transportation Equipment on the outbreak of war.

In 1944, Sir William retired from the post of Chief Mechanical Engineer of the LMS and Fairburn, already the acting chief, became the new CME. Stanier's retirement was followed by another honour, for he was elected to the Fellowship of the Royal Society and thus followed Robert Stephenson, the other locomotive engineer, to become a Fellow of this august society. Although he had retired from railway work

he did not fade into inactive seclusion. He became chairman of a firm developing jet aircraft engines and joined the boards of several other companies. Although over 70 years of age he did not lose interest in locomotive affairs, for he made many speeches and joined in numerous discussions. It was not until he was in his 80s that he became less active.

The early death of Fairburn at the age of 58 led to Ivatt taking over as Chief Mechanical Engineer from January 1946. The building of Stanier-type locomotives had continued on a restricted scale during the war and was carried on after the end of hostilities. Three more 'Duchesses' appeared in 1946, but the end was in sight as far as privately owned railways were concerned, and on 1 January 1948 the railways were nationalised. There was still time before nationalisation for one more 'Duchess' to take the rails, and it was very rightly decided that there could be no better way to acclaim the work of a great engineer than to give his name to the locomotive that marked the ultimate development of steam power on the LMSR. Thus, during the last month of the existence of that railway, there was a ceremony at Euston and No 6256 was named *Sir William Stanier*.

What a pity that No 6256 was broken up so hurriedly after withdrawal in 1964, while other less worthy machines lay rusting in Barry scrapyard and years later were dragged out and restored to their former glory. I feel strongly that No 6256 *Sir William Stanier* should have been preserved and taken its rightful place alongside No 4498 *Sir Nigel Gresley* in the great Steam Cavalcade at Darlington.

The last day of 1947 may have been the end of the LMS, but it was not the end of the influence of Sir William Stanier on steam locomotive design in Britain. Churchward had raised design and performance on the Great Western to levels not previously achieved on a British railway. Stanier had carried these ideals forward to the LMS and developed them to a new peak. The same onward march of these traditions took place when men who had trained and worked under Stanier were chosen to fill most of the posts connected with locomotive design and operation when the nationalised system was formed.

On New Year's Day in 1948 there met for the first time in the former Great Central Hotel at Marylebone, now the headquarters of the Railway Executive, the team which had been appointed to deal with the mechanical and electrical engineering for the national system. R.A. Riddles was the full-time member of the executive for these functions, and R.C. Bond and E. Pugson were the chief officers for locomotive and for carriage & wagon construction and maintenance respectively. Design was a separate function and this was in the hands of E.S. Cox. G.S. Hussey dealt with matters of administration. Other members were G.M. Cock from the Southern Railway, who was in charge of electrical engineering, and A.E.C. Dent of the Great Western, executive officer, road motor engineering. The five first named were all from the LMSR, and thus it may truly be claimed that Sir William Stanier's influence lasted right to the very end of steam traction in Britain.

LMS No 6201 showing the cab details.
G. Allen/6201 PELS

The two prototypes in BR Days. No 46200 *The Princess Royal* and 46201 *Princess Elizabeth* being prepared for passenger duty at Carlisle Kingmoor depot 12 July 1962. *Paul Claxton*

In 1932 the LMS owned no locomotives capable of working 500-ton expresses single-handed throughout the 401-mile Euston–Glasgow run. William Stanier's remit was to produce a design to meet that requirement.

Three Pacifics were ordered on the 1933 locomotive building programme and No 6201's engine history card records this event as follows: 'Charged to renewals, M&EE Minute 142 refers, July 1932'. Almost at once the plan to build three prototypes was changed to two, because the third one was diverted to be built as the non-condensing turbine locomotive No 6202 *Turbomotive*.

Design was underway at the Derby design office, and many stories were circulating at the time, of the intention of William Stanier to 'Westernise' the LMS. The only thing we can say quite definitely, is that the original chimney drawing for No 6201 shows a machined annular groove around the centre, where it was obviously intended to fit another ring. Could this by any chance have been copper? One can only speculate. The idea was obviously quashed, because the draughtsman has tried to erase it, but sufficient has printed through to illustrate the intention.

Drawings were issued rapidly by Derby to Crewe Works, who were intent on showing the 'new man from Swindon' just how well and quickly they could build the new design. Most of our original drawings bear the personal signature 'W.A. Stanier' so it can be safely assumed that he took a personal hand in the design (not like the later 'Coronation' design, when he was away in India at the time Coleman and his team were working on the project).

Nos 6200 and 6201 were built to LMS lot number 99 on Crewe order number 371 at an authorised cost of £9,210. It is interesting that No 6201 also carried a makers number of 107, which is stamped on the motion to this day. No 6200 was completed at Crewe on 27 June 1933, and almost immediately the modifications began – the visible ones were the fitting of an oval plate over the originally round buffers, the height of the vacuum standpipe on the front bufferbeam was twice lowered in height, and even the nameplate was replaced to get the name of *The Princess Royal* right! The locomotive was handed over to traffic on the 1 July 1933 and made its first trip to Glasgow with the 'Royal Scot' train on the 22 September 1933.

Both Pacifics having started work on the Scottish expresses, started to develop faults quickly; the boiler did not steam very well, the superheater temperature was too low and the tender design was unsatisfactory, in that

Top:
Beattock. The down 'Royal Scot' at Harthorpe headed by No 46201.
Eric Treacy/P.B. Whitehouse

Left:
No 46200 *The Princess Royal* passing Harrow in 1951, the scene a year later where No 46202 met her sad demise. *C.R.L. Coles*

Left:
No 6201 fitted with the stove pipe double chimney in 1934. This experiment was never attempted again on a 'Princess Royal'. *NRM/Crown Copyright*

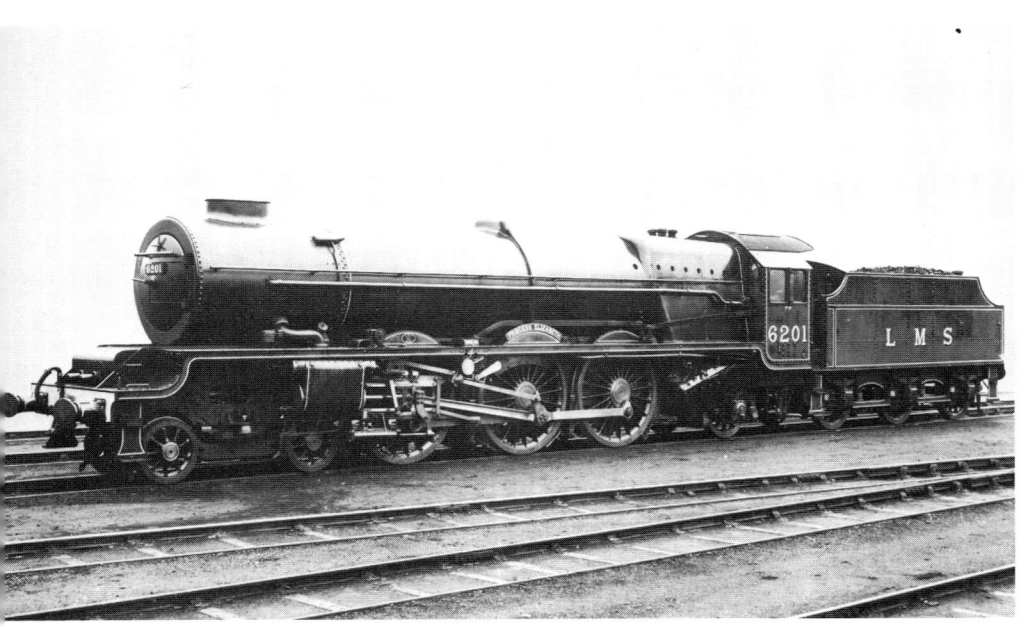

it did not self trim, which proved a nightmare for the fireman at the end of a long run. The poor steaming of the engines resulted in No 6201 being the 'guinea pig' for a disastrous experiment in 1934, the fitting of an unsightly stove pipe double chimney, which gave the locomotive a reputation for being an even worse steamer. This experiment must have shaken the confidence of the design team, for never again did a 'Princess Royal' receive a double chimney.

Nos 6200/6201 and 6202 all appeared originally with domeless boilers. No 6200's original boiler was none too successful and was later replaced, while that on No 6201 was modified, featuring a 32-element superheater (the 16-element version fitted to both Nos 6200 and 6201 at first being inadequate). All the class eventually received the 32-element superheater except of course No 6202 *Turbomotive* (later named *Princess Anne*) which carried a 40-element superheater. However numbers No 6203–06 did carry 24 in an intermediate stage. The small tubes equally had their share of alterations with successively 170, 119, 112, 110 and finally 123 being carried, albeit with different diameters, the length also reduced from 20ft 9in to 19ft 3in with the insertion of a 15in combustion chamber.

The present boiler on No 6201, number 9101, was originally fitted when new to 6203 *Princess Margaret Rose*, and it was not until 1952 that this later pattern could be installed in the two prototypes – the framing was modified and then at long last the 'Princess Royal' class looked similar to each other.

In 1952 the major rebuild of the front end of the frames took place on numbers 6200/01/03/05/11, to be followed by 6206/10 in 1953, and 6207 in 1954.

The last modification to 6201 was carried out in 1958, when the axlebox guides were replaced with a strengthened pattern.

The tenders fitted to Nos 6200 and 6201 were of the established Derby pattern, straight sided six bearings, both tenders of course had a greater water capacity than hitherto – 4,000gal, and 9ton of coal with careful stacking. Later tenders of the same capacity, but with the familiar Stanier curved top were attached behind the engines. However, the deficiencies of these tenders must have been apparent after the record run, undertaken by 6201 in 1936, as 10 days later No 6201 was fitted with tender No 9373 (10ton capacity) and remains behind her to this day. The top being modified after a collision with a coaling plant. In 1936 6200–01 and 6203–12 had all received the new Stanier design 10ton capacity tenders. The only tender which differed of the numbers mentioned, was No 6206 in that it received a steam operated coal pusher.

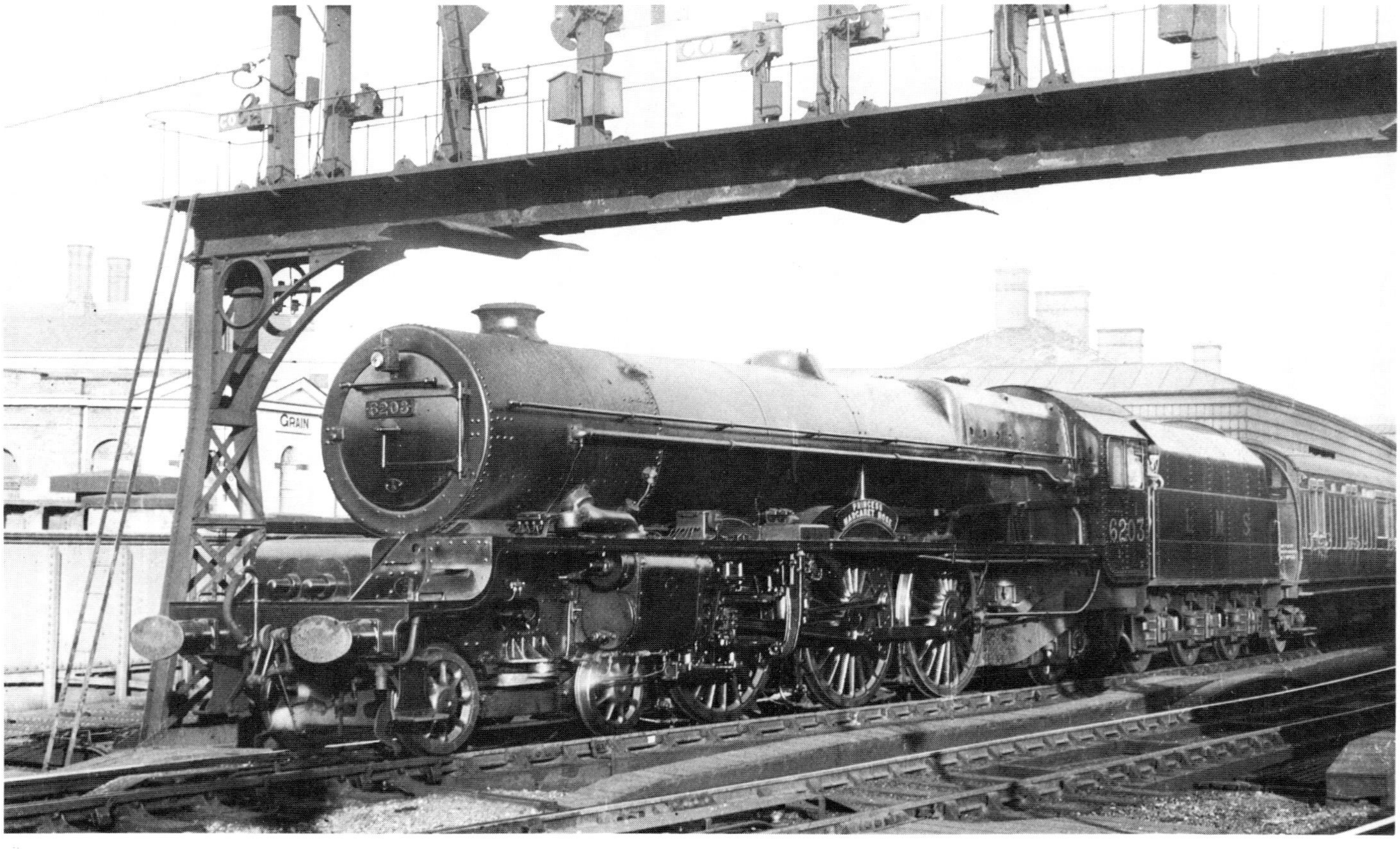

Bottom:
No 6203 *Princess Margaret Rose* on a running-in turn from Crewe, at Shrewsbury in the 1930s, this being the usual section for all 'Princess Royals' to use from the works. Now preserved at Butterley, along with the dynamometer car used in 6201s record runs. *W.H. Whitworth/Rail Archive Stephenson*

The final cost of No 6201 was £11,675 an overspend of some £2,465. It is interesting to note that the new designs must have been considered revolutionary, as the LMS took the unusual step of issuing to motive power depots a 'workshop manual' on the features of the locomotives.

All 'Princess Royals' were painted in LMS Crimson Lake when new, with serif figures in gold leaf shaded in black, this shading was later changed to red. The necessity to repaint in wartime black did not arise, but in 1946 No 6201 appeared in the LMS style of black paint, lined out in maroon and straw. In early British Railways days, after renumbering to 46201, she carried another black livery, this time it was an LNWR form of black, until the 1950s when green was the popular colour. No 6201 missed out on the red revolution of 1958 and so it was left to the society to put back the clock.

Above:
No 46204 *Princess Louise* heads the down 'Merseyside Express' towards Bletchley on 19 May 1955.
D.M.C. Hepburne-Scott/Rail Archive Stephenson

Left:
No 46205 *Princess Victoria* climbs Camden bank with the down 'Merseyside Express' on 9 July 1955, a popular turn for 'Princess Royals'.
D.M.C. Hepburne-Scott/Rail Archive Stephenson

Below:
No 6206, the only 'Princess Royal' fitted with a coal pusher seen at Rugby on the down 'Midday Scot' c1936.
T.G. Hepburn/Rail Archive Stephenson

Top:
No 46207 *Princess Arthur of Connaught* north of Blisworth with the up 'Merseyside Express' on 10 March 1956.
D.M.C. Hepburne-Scott/Rail Archive Stephenson

Above:
No 6208 *Princess Helena Victoria* at Rugby with the down 'Royal Scot' c1938.
T.G. Hepburn/Rail Archive Stephenson

Left:
No 46209 *Princess Beatrice* heads the up 'Midday Scot' near Penrith on 20 May 1956.
D.M.C. Hepburne-Scott/Rail Archive Stephenson

Above right:
No 46210 *Lady Patricia* waits to leave Carlisle Citadel with a Glasgow–Birmingham express on 3 June, 1956.
D.M.C. Hepburne-Scott/Rail Archive Stephenson

Right:
No 6211 *Queen Maud* at Dillicar Troughs on the down 'Royal Scot' 1937.
NRM/Crown Copyright

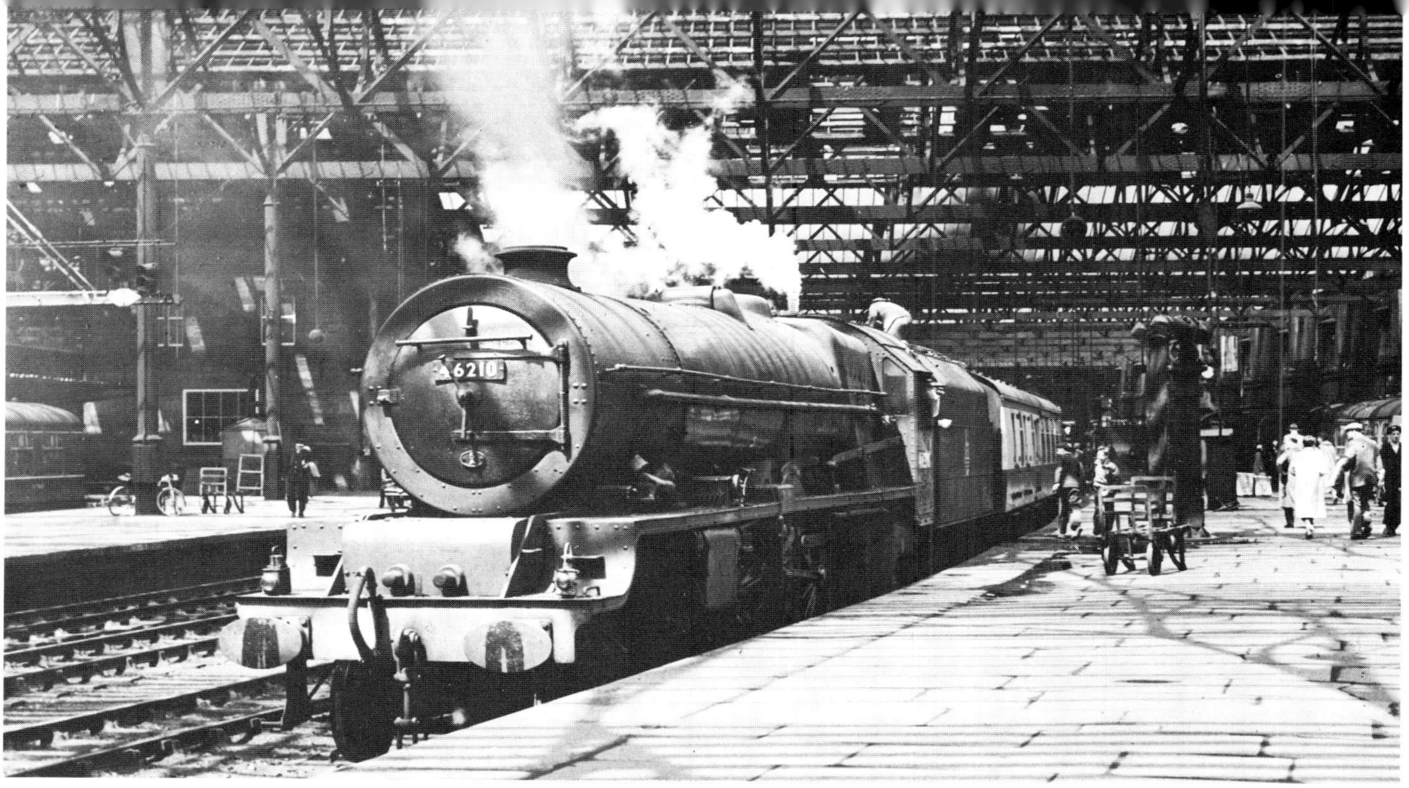
6210

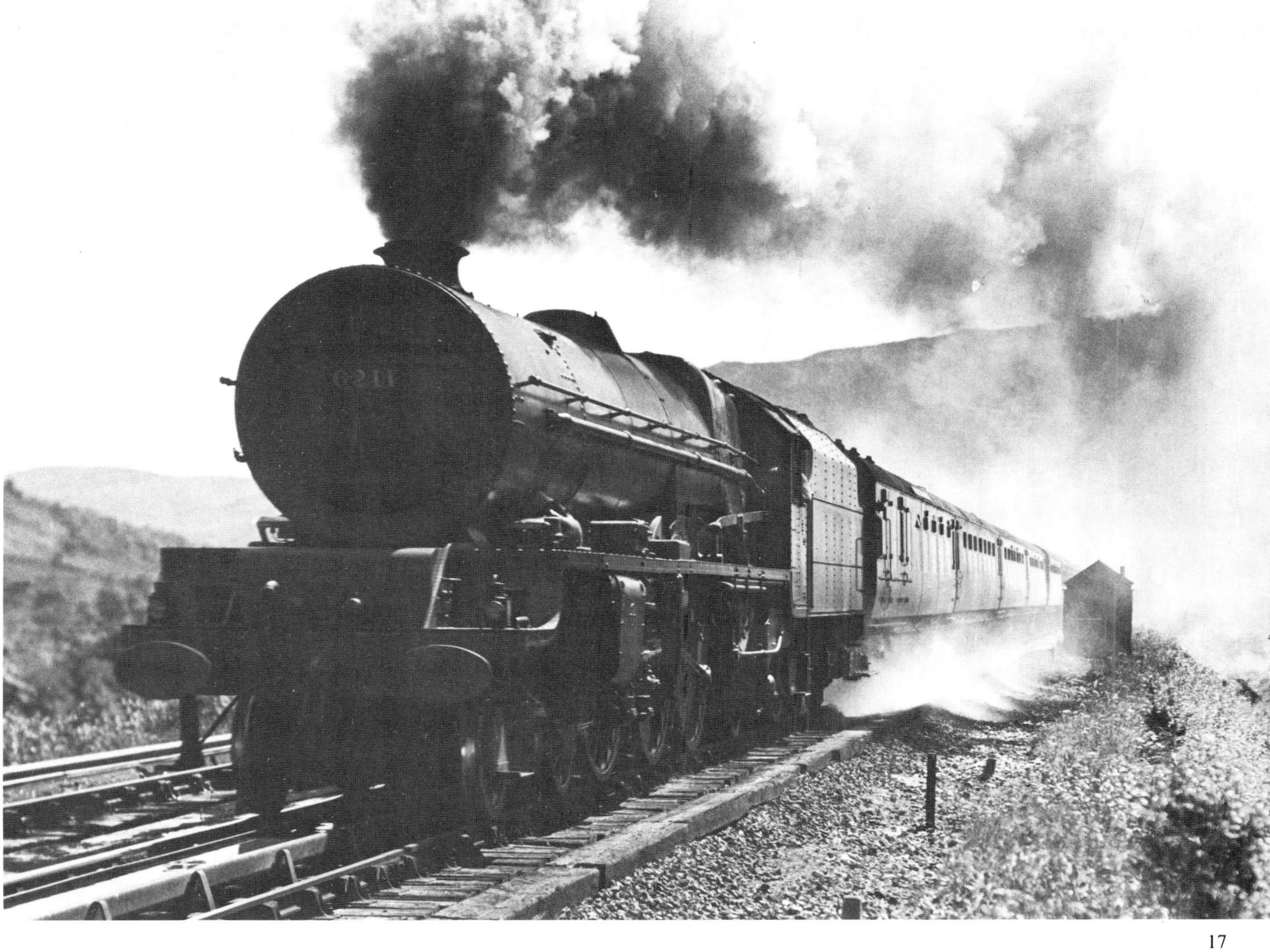

No 46212 *Duchess of Kent* passes Castlemilk sidings with the 11.25am Birmingham–Glasgow express on 11 May 1956. Castlemilk sidings, where No 6201 in 1936 achieved a minimum of 75mph on the first leg of her record run.
D.M.C. Hepburne-Scott/Rail Archive Stephenson

Above:
No 46202 on the 8.30am Euston–Liverpool near Carpenders Park, May 1949, fitted with smoke deflectors after exhaust steam was found to be obscuring the cab. *Rev. B. Whitworth/IAL*

Below:
No 6202 under repair at Crewe in the 1930s. *W.H. Whitworth/Rail Archive Stephenson*

No 6202

Although No 6202 was included in the 1933 building programme, and became a non-condensing turbine locomotive, it did not appear in traffic until June 1935.

Metropolitan Vickers were the company to put the turbines into the frames, the rest of the locomotive being completed at Crewe Works. Smoke deflectors were fitted after entering service later due to the obscuring of the cab windows by exhaust steam.

The general view of this design was that it would need less intermediate servicing, thus increasing locomotive availability, plus advantages of reduced coal and water consumption. On dynamometer tests between Euston–Glasgow in 1936–37 it gave encouragement to the engineers, that it could be even more succesful than the rest of the 'Princess Royal' class. The rest of its service was however to be concentrated on the Euston–Liverpool route. It was in traffic from 1935–1939, withdrawn until July 1941 when it was required again for war use. It had been stored in the meantime at Crewe Works, withdrawn again for a time between 1943–44 and eventually in March 1950. The locomotive was then dismantled and a decision was taken by BR to rebuild No 6202 as near as possible to a conventional Pacific. It left Crewe Works in June 1952 as No 46202 *Princess Anne*, only to be involved on 8 October, the same year, in the tragic Harrow & Wealdstone railway disaster; the capabilities of the locomotive never to be fully realised.

No 6201 in LMS Days

Leaving Crewe Works on 3 November 1933, No 6201 *Princess Elizabeth* was officially allocated to Camden shed as from the next day, but instead worked between Crewe and Carlisle until 18 November, arriving at Camden for duty on 20 November. The use of the name *Princess Elizabeth* required regal approval and so the nameplates were not at first fitted. On 22 November, with indicator shelter in place, No 6201 worked the down 'Royal Scot'.

During 1936, No 6201 achieved a commendable mileage run of 83,320 despite a heavy overhaul. Such a mileage underlined the ability of the locomotive, while the record runs that November, brought the LMS much-needed publicity. Indeed, the times between Euston and Glasgow Central achieved by No 6201 were never improved upon by steam traction – 5hr 53min northbound, 9½min faster back to Euston. No 6201 settled down to the Euston–Glasgow run after her moment of glory, running 77,789 and 78,704 miles respectively in 1937 and 1938, no small achievement when measured against the later 'Duchess' design. The war years and the lack of effective maintenance inevitably took their toll, 1943 bringing an all time low, when only 30,340 miles were run with 176 days being spent out of service for repairs.

Initially allocated to Camden, No 6201 saw service from Glasgow Polmadie, Longsight, Edge Hill, Crewe North, Carlisle Kingmoor and Carlisle Upperby sheds – the last being its final home in BR service.

Below:
The 'Royal Scot' at Bushey hauled by No 6201 *Princess Elizabeth* with Fowler tender.
Real Photos

Bottom left:
A view of No 6201 under construction in Crewe works 16 August 1933.
BBC Hulton Picture Library

Bottom right:
No 6201 fitted with oval buffers but retaining original tender, on the 'Royal Scot' near Grayrigg in 1934. *H. Gordon Tidey/IAL*

Top left:
Partially dismantled in the shops at Crewe Works and carrying the boiler with which it made the famed record breaking run from Euston–Glasgow and return in November 1936. *W.H. Whitworth/Rail Archive Stephenson*

Above left:
Taking water at Dillicar troughs, No 6201 hauls the down 'Royal Scot' in 1936. The new Stanier tender having been fitted after the dynamometer car tests on 16/17 November. *NRM/Crown Copyright*

Left:
No 6201 on the down 'Royal Scot' at Beattock 1937, scene of one of the locomotive's exploits on the record run the previous year. *NRM/Crown Copyright*

Top:
The down 'Midday Scot' hauled by No 6201 at South Kenton c1937 with Stanier tender. *NRM/Crown Copyright*

Above:
No 6201 *Princess Elizabeth* heads a Rugby–Euston train between Cheddington and Tring in 1937. The formation also includes milk tanks and van at the rear. *F.R. Hebron/Rail Archive Stephenson*

Right:
In postwar LMS livery of black edged in maroon and straw, No 6201 runs light through Crewe c1947. *W.H. Whitworth/Rail Archive Stephenson*

Nationalisation as No 46201

On the 12 March 1961, the engine was transferred on loan from the Scottish Region but was actually placed into store at Carlisle (Kingmoor), the effects of dieselisation were now being felt. This period of storage in a serviceable condition lasted until 22 January 1962, when, much to everyones surprise, the nameplates were put back on and 'Lizzie' began her 'Indian summer' on main line duty. At this time six of the 'Princess Royals' were already withdrawn and being gathered at Crewe South shed for scrapping in the works.

However, on 2 June 1962, two railway societies, the Stephenson Locomotive Society and the RCTS had organised a special train from London to Aberdeen, to mark the end of steam haulage of the principal East Coast Anglo-Scottish expresses. This special was called the 'Aberdeen Flyer' and the locomotives chosen for the run north were 'A4s' *Mallard* and *William Whitelaw*. Coming south via the West Coast main line the honours fell to the two prototype Stanier Pacifics *The Princess Royal* and *Princess Elizabeth*. Aboard this train were Peter Handford, the Argo and Transacord teams who subsequently produced an EP and two LPs of No 6201 at work from Aberdeen with 407ton trailing. This remains a tribute in sound, to work carried out for British Railways in the twilight of her career.

Duties in 1962 also included hauling parcels and fish trains from Carlisle to Perth, but a passenger working, the 9.50am Euston–Perth was added. Visits to Edinburgh were undertaken, with the engine bringing the 2.25pm train from Waverley into Perth on 14 July. In fact the authorities were said to be interested in making greater use of the class, to offset the uncertainties of the North British Locomotive Type two diesels! Despite this, No 6201 was again placed in store with the start of the winter timetables. The nameplates were removed on 10 September 1962, again at Carlisle.

In all her service *Princess Elizabeth* had amassed a mileage totalling 1,526,807. The engine record card states that she was withdrawn as being 'outside authorised programme' on 20 October 1962, and further notes that on 12 February 1963 she was sold to Mr Bell of the Elizabethan Society!

Top right:
British Railways ownership shows No 46201 with the approved new design of crest.
6201 PELS

Centre right:
On a Glasgow–Birmingham working, No 46201 at Clifton near Penrith. *Eric Treacy*

Above right:
Polmadie – where No 46201 was shedded at one time, shows the locomotive only just able to fit on to the turntable, c1959.
NRM/Crown Copyright

Right:
A contrast of two classes of Stanier locomotives – Nos 45724 *Warspite* and 46201 *Princess Elizabeth* at Carlisle Citadel, waiting to take forward trains for Perth and Glasgow. *Eric Treacy*

Top:
The locomotive hauls a Liverpool express in 1949 at Bushey. *Real Photos (24230)*

Centre:
With 14 on, No 46201 passes Watford in 1950, in grimy condition. *Real Photos (24152)*

Above:
No 46201 working a down Merseyside express passing Kenton, in July 1959. This was one of my own favourite places in train spotting days. *C.R.L. Coles*

Left:
A down 'Midday Scot' at Tring on 25 August 1953 hauled by No 46201.
NRM/Crown Copyright

Left:
The Glasgow–Birmingham express passing Carstairs No 2 box with No 46201 on September 25, 1955.
D.M.C. Hepburne-Scott/Rail Archive Stephenson

Below left:
Locomotive and train at Carstairs waiting to continue on to Birmingham, 25 September 1955.
D.M.C. Hepburne-Scott/Rail Archive Stephenson

Below right:
No 46201 climbing Shap, echoing its past historic 1936 run near Greenholme 26 May 1958. *G.W. Morrison*

Bottom:
Empty stock for the Glasgow Central–Birmingham, passes St Rollox shed behind No 46201, due to Sunday closure of Central station on 12 April 1959. *G.W. Morrison*

Left:
The 10.20 Warrington Bank Quay–Glasgow Central at Grayrigg hauled by No 46201 on 30 July 1960. *J.E. Wilkinson*

Below:
Stored at Carlisle Kingmoor, May 1961 before being eventually put back into service on 22 January 1962. *G.W. Morrison*

Above:
2 July 1962 at Ferryhill the locomotive is ready for working the SLS and RCTS special train to mark the end of steam haulage of the principal East Coast Anglo-Scottish expresses. *6201 PELS*

Above right:
On shed at Kingmoor 29 April 1962, this was to be No 46201's last year in BR service. *6201 PELS*

Right:
No 46201 hauled not only passenger but fish and meat trains. This photograph shows the locomotive on a Sunday train in August 1962, at Hilton Junction. *W.J.V. Anderson*

An Indian Summer

Left:
Leaving Carstairs junction with a Birmingham–Glasgow express in 1962. *D. Anderson*

Below:
On Beattock 1962 with the up 'Midday Scot'. *D. Anderson*

Right:
Beattock is tackled yet again on a Birmingham–Glasgow working in 1962. *D. Anderson*

Below right:
No 46201 at work on Beattock bank in 1962. *D. Anderson*

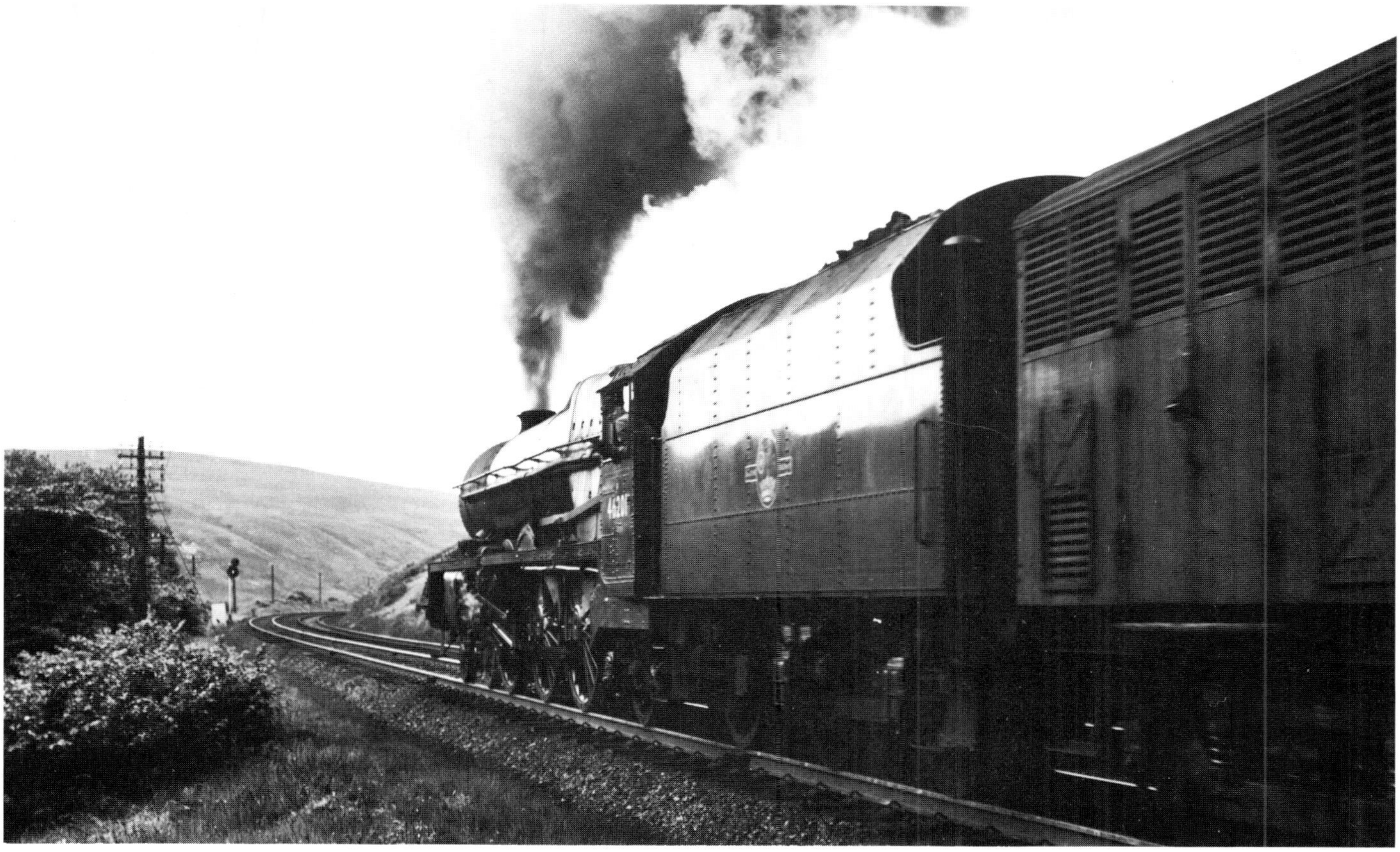

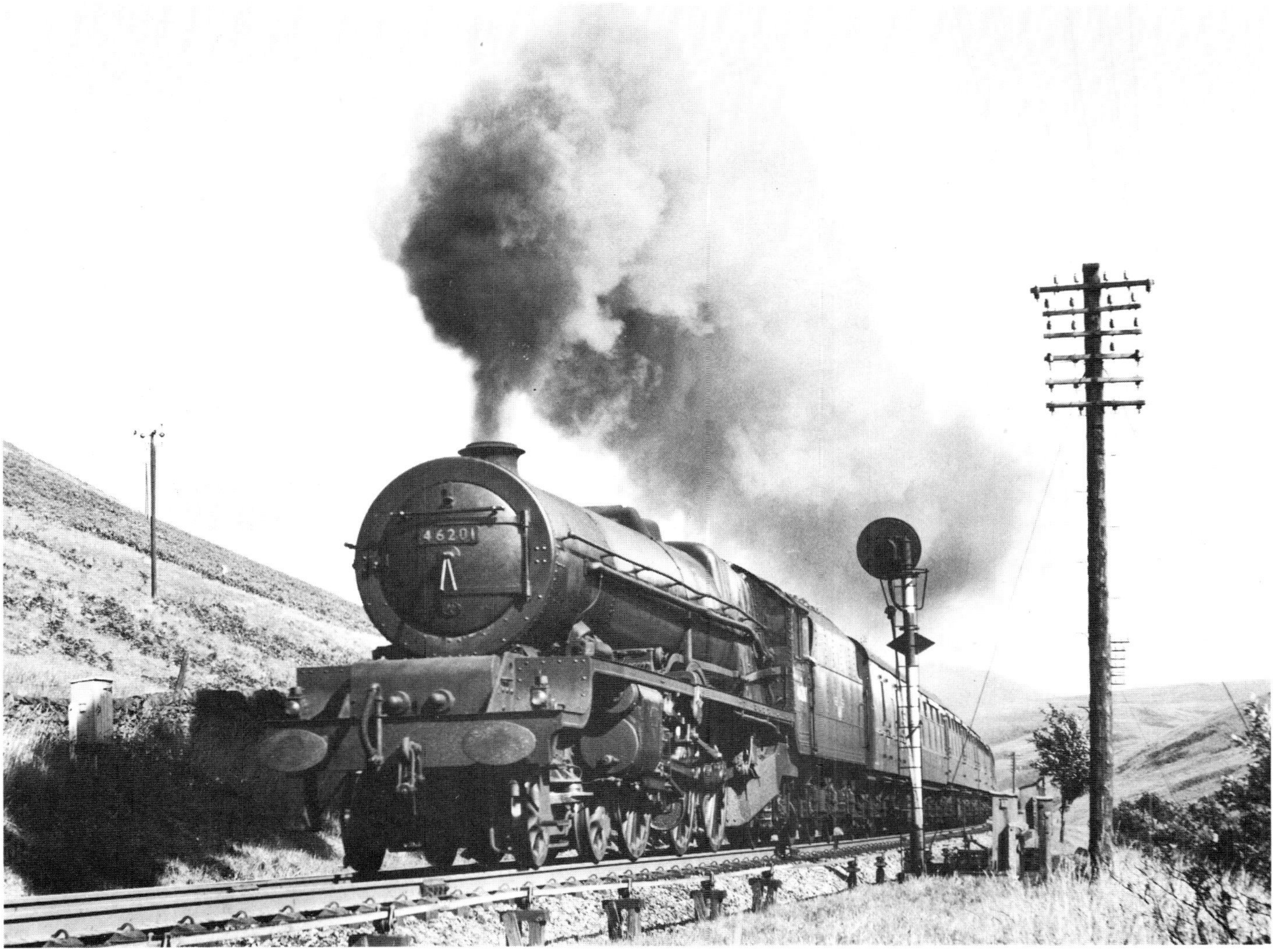

The Record

Before the exploits of No 6201 in 1936, the locomotive had in fact been involved in tests from Crewe to Carlisle on 17 December 1933. A special empty stock train weighing 502ton was run, including Dynamometer Car No 1. Leaving Crewe at 9.00am and returning from Carlisle at 1.25pm the locomotive was worked with Grimethorpe coal, the same to be used in 1936. However this test run was unheralded and actual times were generally overdue, because of delays due to fog on the return to Crewe. Sectional times were however kept well by the locomotive, and the climb up Shap bank was made in 8min 23sec, against a booked time of 11min. The locomotive was even at this stage never extended, the maximum cut off used being 40%.

So to the events of 1936.

On 16/17 November 1936 a return non-stop test run was arranged to assess the needs of the high-speed services planned for 1937. It was also undertaken to find out the capabilities of the 'Princess Royals' between

London–Glasgow, and how standard coaching stock would respond to sustained non-stop running.

William Stanier was in India, so E.J.H. Lemon was responsible for the arrangements. Among his team were D.C. Urie (superintendent of motive power), H.G. Ivatt (divisional mechanical engineer, Glasgow), and R.A. Riddles (principal assistant to CME) who rode on the footplate, with the continuous diagram of all speed restrictions to be observed around his neck. This he unrolled as the journey progressed.

The driver chosen for the test run was T.J. Clark, fireman T. Fleet, passed fireman A. Shaw (all of Crewe), locomotive inspector S.E. Miller (Willesden) and guard F. Howes (Euston). It is said that driver Laurie Earl of Camden was upset at not being chosen for the turn.

The locomotive chosen for the test run was No 6201 Princess Elizabeth, which had run 77,096 miles since its last general repair, and 1,612 miles since the last service repair. A standby locomotive was required, so initially

No 6210 was chosen, but subsequently changed to No 6203 Princess Margaret Rose. No 6201 was stopped at Willesden on 15 November to be made ready for the following day. However when the locomotive was checked it was found to have a leaking joint in the main steampipe. This had to be repaired, so an urgent message was sent to R.C. Bond at Crewe to unearth a spare ring from the works. This was found after some difficulty (Crewe Works stores being shut) and handed to the driver of the 6.40pm up train with instructions that it should only be delivered to R. Riddles on the platform, when he arrived at Euston. It took most of the night to repair the locomotive, but by morning all was ready.

Below:
Checking the dynamometer car equipment before leaving Euston on 16 November 1936. *Fox Photos*

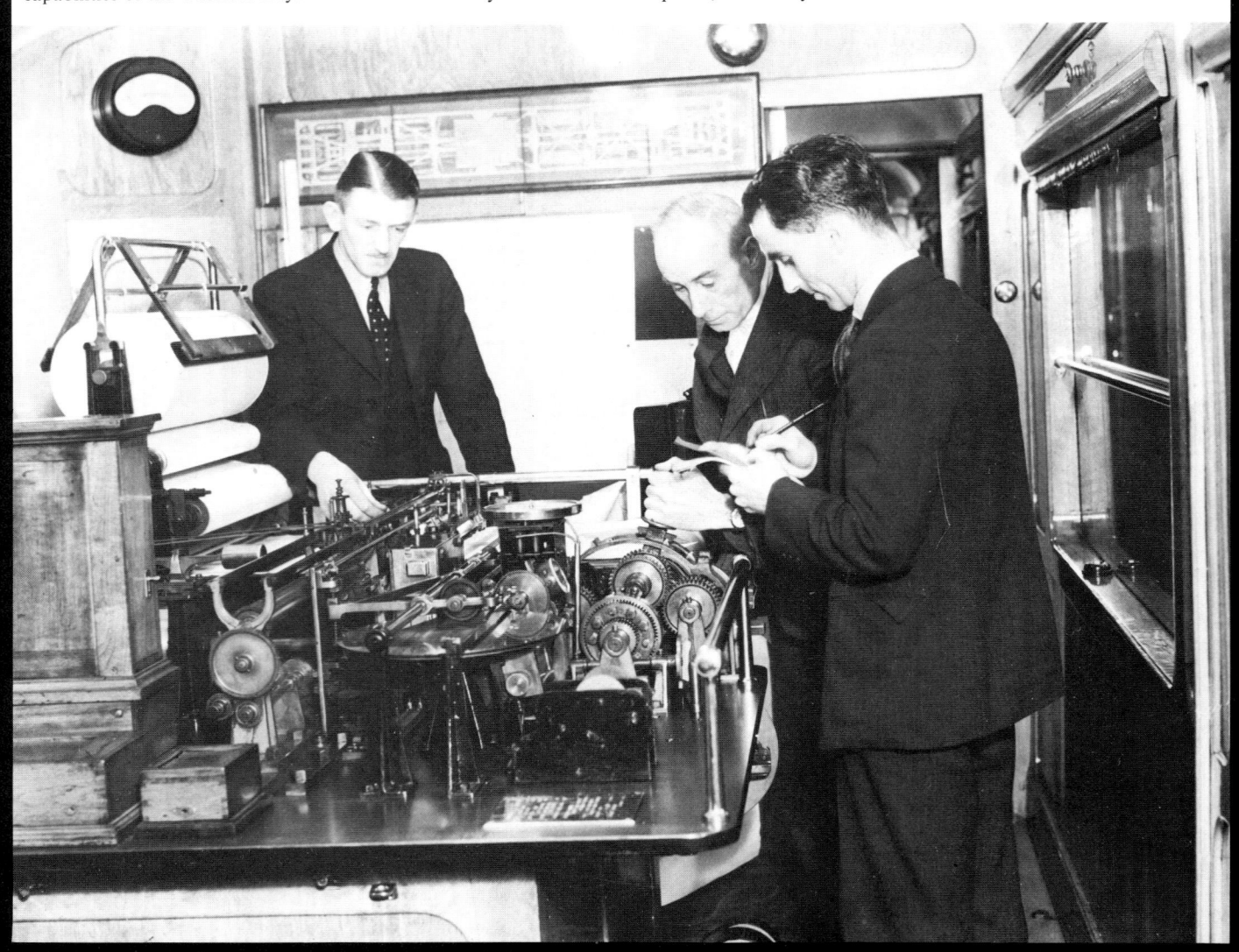

The test train was made up of seven coaches weighing a total of 225 tons, consisting dynamometer car, brake composite, corridor first, vestibule first, kitchen car, vestibule third and brake third. Given a schedule of six hours to Glasgow, this load was similar to the London & North Eastern's (Silver Jubilee) train.

Train 703 left Euston at 9.50am, 10 minutes ahead of the 'Royal Scot', and due to reach Glasgow (Central) 115 minutes ahead of it. By the time Willesden was reached the train had reached 66mph, but had to slow for a permanent way restriction at Wembley. However between Tring and Bletchley, driver and fireman were now working the engine to some of the highest speeds of the outward journey (95.75mph). At every station, bridge or vantage point along the route, crowds gathered to watch and cheer No 6201's progress, many of them being LMS employees, anxious to see the LNER 'Silver Jubilee' train exploits improved upon.

Some 50 or more speed restrictions had to be observed on the run, and the continuous diagram which Mr Riddles had, saw that this was done in conjunction with his crew. A typical example of restrictions of the train was at Betley Road, some 4¾ miles from Crewe, speed being 90mph, but Crewe itself was taken at 20mph. On platform 2 a crowd of retired drivers shouted encouragement to the crew, who were leaning from the cab. Fast acceleration within 7½ miles saw 85mph attained. Already it was proving that the locomotive's acceleration was never in doubt. However the challenge to a fine crew was yet to come, in the form of Shap and Beattock. Yet these were achieved seemingly with ease. Tebay to Shap Summit was completed at an average of 64.5mph, and speed at the summit was 57.0, some 916ft above sea level. The locomotive and train took the incline with ease. Driver Clark had to actually apply the brakes going up, something which had never happened before.

Soon after the descent from Shap Fell levelling out near Carlisle, Driver Clark and his crew were preparing for the second steep ascent – Beattock 1,014ft above sea level. Carlisle to Floriston some 6 miles, saw speed rise from 20 to 85½mph. A slack at Gretna junction was followed by 70mph for seven miles at 1 in 200, with a minimum of 75mph on the four mile climb to Castlemilk Siding. More fast running saw the 10 miles from Beattock Station to the Summit (average gradient 1 in 75) reached in 9min 31sec. A minimum of 56mph was attained and the summit was topped at 58mph. At Beattock Station the staff having put a large notice up stating 'It's in your pocket'.

Glasgow 401.4 miles from London, had been reached in 353min 38sec at an average

Top right:
Driver T.J. Clark and Fireman T. Fleet before they left Euston on the first leg of the record run. *Fox Photos*

Right:
No 6201 leaves Euston with the special 703 headboard 16 November 1936. *Fox Photos*

speed of 68.1mph, and a gain on the original schedule of 6½min.

So the outstanding features of the test train were the high average speed, plus the exceptional hill climbing allied to the rapid acceleration from the speed restrictions. And this was only the first half of the journey.

Driver Clark praised his fine crew on arrival at Glasgow, and said the locomotive could have exceeded 100mph. The footplate crew were congratulated by Mr J. Ballantyne (chief officer for Scotland) and other officers of the LMSR. That evening the crew were entertained at a dinner to celebrate the run, Mr Lemon presiding. In reply to a toast to the crew Driver Clark responded: 'I was asked on Friday if I could do this job. I said I could. I was asked on Saturday if I would do it. I said I would. Today I have done it.' As one commentator observed, it would not do for politicians to be like Driver Clark – to say so little, and to do so much!

However, yet again, drama was to take place at the dinner that evening, although no one was aware of this except Riddles, who was handed a note from Polmadie shed, stating that the left outside crosshead slipper had run hot, and lost its white metal. Fortunately Lemon said that Riddles looked tired, so seemingly he retired to bed. But in fact had sent a reply already, that the engine should be got to St Rollox. Riddles immediately went to St Rollox, where they worked through the night to complete the repair, so that the engine was ready for its return journey the next day.

Glasgow–Euston 17 November 1936
The return journey was to be undertaken in conditions of torrential rain accompanied by gusting high winds. An added penalty was the extra coach, on Riddles suggestion which made the total tare weight of 255 tons. In Riddles opinion the engine had already proved itself.

Train 703 left Glasgow at 1.20pm 10 minutes in advance of the 'Mid-Day Scot', and despite permanent way slacks managed to regain time, with a rapid climb to Beattock Summit. Speed at the summit was a remarkable 70mph.

Shap was also taken at the same speed. Despite a two minute deficit at Carstairs, the fast running meant that at Preston the train was five minutes early, six minutes at Wigan and nine minutes at Warrington. For a distance of six miles between Winsford and Coppenhall Junctions the train maintained an average of 90mph, with a maximum of 95. It was dark when the engine reached its birthplace at Crewe, still nine minutes early. Again the station saw enthusiastic crowds lining the platforms.

As before acceleration was the highlight of the return journey. A colliery subsidence at Polesworth meant the speed was down to 30mph but in 4.2 miles had again risen to 79 at Atherstone with adverse grades. The 15-mile ascent of the Chiltern Hills was covered in 11min 3sec (average 81.7mph) despite the weather conditions being extremely bad. Near Watford the world's record beater slowing for a restriction, was passed by a local electric train. So much for fame.

Cheering greeted the train as it arrived at Euston, where after being congratulated by Sir Josiah Stamp (chairman of the LMSR) and other officials, the crew were carried shoulder high from the station. The reception at Euston was more reminiscent of a film star, rather than of a locomotive crew, with brilliant floodlights being erected on the platform.

Broadcast at the BBC
That evening the crew were invited to Broadcasting House of the BBC, and interviewed for the national news. Asked if the locomotive had had any special treatment, Driver Clark replied: 'No. The

only extra piece of equipment added on to the locomotive was a speedometer.' In typically modest fashion, when asked if they would be breaking any more records, driver and fireman replied that they would be back doing their usual turns of duty between Crewe, Carlisle and London. They all agreed that the broadcast was more nerve-wracking than breaking records. In fireman Fleet's instance, he received a cheque for £2-2s-0d (£2.10), which was passed on to him by the chief operating manager, Euston House, for his part in the radio interview.

The clock presentation

On 25 November 1936 a presentation was made to all of the crew involved in the previous week's exploits. This was in the form of a clock duly inscribed, recording particulars of the record run. Sir Josiah Stamp in making the presentations, referred to 'an LMS job well done', and to the great interest which the record runs had aroused among public and staff alike. The photograph of one of these clocks is shown, and remarkably still in working order.

Driver Clark became something of a national hero, appearing in the Honours list of 1937. The locomotive was modelled in 'O' gauge by at least two manufacturers and Driver Clark's statement in the advertising material for Hornby was 'she's fine'.

Reflections

The publicity that the LMS gained from the record runs had put them once again in the forefront of steam operation worldwide. This was besides the valuable information gained of high speed working, and its effect on train regulation and signalbox working. The crew had shown that it was the high speed up the banks, and not the reckless running down them which were the key to success. Smooth running was highlighted by the dining-car attendant, walking down the corridor with trays of tea and coffee piled high, seemingly unconcerned, despite the train travelling at 90mph down the Chiltern slopes. Above all it was a team effort by all concerned.

Fireman Fleet

Driver Clark when asked who he wanted as his fireman for the test run, said 'the little fellow'. Fireman Fleet (being the little fellow) was a very unassuming man, although well known for his humour in the 'Earl of Crewe'.

Living near to his job at Crewe, Fireman Fleet and his family lived and breathed railways. In the 1930s a crew's turn would consist of 8 hours on and 12 off, seven days a week, so there were no weekends off for the family as such. The children would be constantly reminded to be quiet as Dad was in bed, and if one asked when he was on work, no one knew until the 'knocker up' came, which could be sometimes in the middle of the night.

The 'knocker up' was not a well-liked person, but because there were no telephones for poorer families, he had a job to do. When the 'knocker up' came, he would give the fireman (in this case) a slip of paper to tell him what time to book on. On this occasion fireman Fleet had asked his wife for his

			LMSR Euston—Glasgow Central			
			Non-Stop Test Runs			
			DOWN: 16th November, 1936 *Load: 7 coaches, 225 tons tare, 230 tons gross*		*UP: 17 November, 1936* *Load: 8 coaches, 255 tons tare, 260 tons gross*	
Dist miles	Sched min	Times min sec		Dist miles	Sched min	Times min sec
0·00	0	0 00	EUSTON	401·35	360	344 15
5·40	8	7 24	WILLESDEN JUNCTION .	395·95	352	335 45
		pws				pws
17·45	18	18 55	WATFORD JUNCTION .	383·90	342	325 38
31·65	30	29 55	Tring . . .	369·70	331	315 30
46·65	41	40 32	BLETCHLEY . .	354·70	318	304 27
59·90	51	50 53	Roade . . .	341·45	308	294 33
69·70	—	62 46	Weedon . .	331·65	—	287 08
82·55	70	68 33	RUGBY* . .	318·80	289	276 05
97·10	82	81 08	NUNEATON . .	304·25	277	264 33
110·00	95	92 53	TAMWORTH . .	291·35	264	252 58
116·25	100	97 38	Lichfield . .	285·10	259	248 37
124·30	106	103 36	Rugeley . .	277·05	253	242 25
133·55	114	111 52	STAFFORD* . .	267·80	245	233 46
147·65	127	123 47	Whitmore . .	253·70	233	222 53
158·00	136	132 52	CREWE* . .	243·35	223	213 17
174·30	149	146 00	*Weaver Junction* .	227·05	209	200 37
182·15	156	153 30	WARRINGTON .	219·20	202	193 34
193·90	168	164 55	WIGAN . .	207·45	190	182 42
197·15	171½	168 30	*Standish Junction* .	204·20	186½	179 58
203·55	177	173 36	Euxton Junction .	197·80	—	174 42
209·00	183	179 15	PRESTON* . .	192·35	175	168 55
218·50	191½	188 05	Garstang . .	182·85	167	161 00
230·00	200	196 35	LANCASTER . .	171·35	158	152 07
236·25	205	201 28	CARNFORTH . .	165·10	153	147 12
243·55	—	206 45	Milnthorpe . .	157·80	—	141 45
249·10	215	211 38	OXENHOLME . .	152·25	143	137 18
256·15	—	218 04	Grayrigg . .	145·20	—	131 22
262·10	227	223 06	Tebay . .	139·25	132	126 15
267·55	233	228 12	*Shap Summit* .	133·80	127	121 50
281·25	245	240 05	PENRITH . .	120·10	114	109 15
294·30	—	250 00	Wreay . .	107·05	—	99 12
299·10	260	255 24	CARLISLE* . .	102·25	97	93 20
307·70	268	263 27	Gretna Junction .	93·65	90	86 10
315·70	—	270 38	Kirtlebridge . .	85·65	—	79 55
324·75	282	277 40	LOCKERBIE . .	76·60	77	72 49
338·70	293	287 35	Beattock . .	62·65	66	62 29
348·70	306	297 06	*Beattock Summit* .	52·65	57	54 20
351·60	—	299 26	Elvanfoot . .	49·75	—	51 57
362·20	—	309 25	Lamington† . .	39·15	—	43 17
365·90	—	313 15	SYMINGTON . .	35·45	—	40 35
372·60	328	319 30	CARSTAIRS* . .	28·75	33	34 30
377·55	—	324 44	*Craigenhill Summit* .	23·80	—	30 16
383·10	338	329 38	LAW JUNCTION* .	18·25	22	24 30
		pws				pws
388·50	344	336 34	MOTHERWELL* . .	12·85	16	16 50
		pws				pws
394·75	—	344 03	Newton . .	6·60	—	9 05
		pws				pws
401·35	360	353 38	GLASGOW CENTRAL .	0·00	0	0 00

*Speed restriction.   †Severe slack, down journey only.

railway uniform cap, which he seldom wore, she being unaware at this stage of anything different than a double trip working being undertaken. (A double trip was Crewe–London–Crewe, a single trip Crewe–Warrington). His usual 'grub' basket to carry his meal in was made up, and he set off for duty as normal. Not until the next day when

the children had arrived home from school. did the family realise that one half of the record run had been completed. Amidst great excitement they were told that 'Dad' would not be home, as he was in Scotland, to try for a faster time the next day. The family were all taken down to Crewe to see special train 703 pass through, and one of the

children remarked: 'But mum, he did not stop to talk to us.'

On arriving home they were advised to switch on the radio for the BBC news. The interview was with the jubilant locomotive crew.

The next day the children were given a day off from school, not however, before they had stood up in assembly, and been cheered by the rest of the school.

North Shed Crewe, was a formidable place, and it was well known that the residents in the area would not hang out washing due to smoke and steam coming from the place.

By the time World War 2 had begun fireman Fleet had been passed out as a driver and was in the 'Top Link' working trains throughout the 'Blitz', the crew never knew whether they would be confronted with bomb craters, or indeed come under attack at any time.

Being conscientious, and proud of their locomotives, most drivers would book on at least one hour early to oil up, fill the sandboxes and usually had a favourite duster for final polishing of brasswork. The drivers used to have their own locomotives allocated to them, and would generally sulk if they had to have another man's locomotive. With the rivalry that existed between the different railway companies, they were certainly a breed of men apart.

Extract from *British Pacific Locomotives*

By Cecil J. Allen

One of the finest runs that I ever noted personally behind an engine of this class was on the down 'Royal Scot; in the early part of 1937, when that master of his craft, Laurie A. Earl, was in charge, with fireman Abey, of No. 6206 *Princess Marie Louise*. We had a big train of sixteen vehicles, 492 tons tare and 515 tons with passengers and luggage. I had been incautious enough to show my face in the vicinity of the footplate shortly before starting from Euston, and this was the result. In Table I the times and speeds between Euston and Rugby are set out in detail. We were delayed in the earlier stage of the run, though even so it was obvious that the engine had no difficulty in maintaining a mile a minute up the long stretches of 1 in 335 before Tring.

The running then became spectacular indeed. After two maxima of 85mph down the 1 in 333 before Bletchley, we swept up a similar grade to Roade at a minimum of 72½mph; and a top speed of 79mph on but little easier than level track to Weedon was followed by a minimum of 70½mph at Kilsby Tunnel. From Tring to Hillmorton, just before slowing down to the Rugby stop, a distance of 48·6 miles was covered at an average speed of 77·2mph – and this with a 515-ton train! The net time over the 82·6 miles from Euston to Rugby was 79min; and though the running on to Crewe was a little less spectacular, a net non-stop time of 150min from Euston to Crewe would have been a matter of little difficulty.

It may be added that Earl, as usual, was keeping the regulator of *Princess Marie Louise* wide open for most of the way up to Tring, with 30% cut-off up Camden bank, 25% from Camden to Willesden, 20% as far as the Berkhamsted check, and 30% in recovering from there up to Tring. From Tring onwards, the opening varied between 20% downhill and level, and 25% on the 1 in 330 climbs to Roade and to Kilsby Tunnel.

One of the hardest tasks ever imposed on 'Princess Royal' Pacifics was during the years immediately preceding the introduction of the 'Coronation Scot', when the down 'Midday Scot', heavily loaded by the inclusion of through portions from Liverpool and Manchester, was booked to cover the 51·25 miles from Lancaster over Shap summit to Penrith in 59min start to stop, and this with a load which might rise to 15 and even 16 coaches . The best run that I timed during that period is set out in Table 2, when No. 6209 *Princess Beatrice,* with a fourteen-coach train of 448 tons tare and 470 tons gross, made the run in 56min 24sec. It will be noted that the minimum speed up the 2½ miles at 1 in 134 beyond Carnforth was 60mph; that the long climb of 12·6 miles from Milnthorpe to Grayrigg was completed in 14min 45sec, with a minimum of 40½mph on the final 2 miles at 1 in 106; and that the 5·6 miles from Tebay to Shap summit, mostly at 1 in 75, were run in 8min 22sec.

As to the improvement in efficiency of the 'Princess Royal' Pacifics resulting from their equipment with 32-element superheaters, a run in 1935 with the 5.25pm from Liverpool to Euston by No 6200 *The Princess Royal* gives ample proof. With a fifteen-coach train of 453 tons tare and 475 tons gross the 152·6 miles from Crewe to Willesden Junction were run in 129min 33sec start to stop. Apart from the usual speed restrictions at Stafford and Rugby, the only other slack was over the pitfall at Polesworth. Highlights of the performance were the drop only from 60 to 57¾mph up the 1 in 177 of Madeley bank, and the time of 12min 33sec for the 15·0 miles from Bletchley up to Tring, with an absolute minimum of 67mph; maximum speeds were 80½mph at Standon Bridge, 80 beyond Rugeley, 85½ at Hademore, 82 at Brinklow, 85½ at Weedon, 82 at Castlethorpe, 86½ at Kings Langley and 85½ at Wembley; the 67·25 miles from Welton to Wembley took no more than 52min 17sec, for an average of 77·2mph.

Three days later No 6200 made a test run with a 461-ton special train, which included the dynamometer car, from Crewe to Glasgow and back. Minimum speeds going north were 43mph at Grayrigg and 35 at Shap summit, while the 10 miles at 1 in 88–69 from Beattock up to Beattock summit were completed without the speed falling below 30mph. Coming south, a very fast run was made over the 66·9 miles from Symington to Carlisle in 59min 41sec; after that 45mph was attained up the 1 in 132 from Carlisle to Wreay, and on the long 1 in 125 up to Shap the lowest rate was 49mph. Yet all this was done on a coal consumption of 52·6lb/mile, which worked out at an average of 2·88lb/drawbar-hp/hr, *The Princess Royal* thus tying with the high efficiency figure attained by the Great Western Railway's 4-6-0 *Caldicot Castle* nine years earlier.

Table 1
LMSR Euston–Rugby
Engine: 4-6-2 No 6206 *Princess Marie Louise*
Load: 16 coaches, 492 tons tare, 515 tons gross

Dist miles		*Sched* min	*Actual* min sec	*Speeds* mph
0·00	EUSTON . . .	0	0 00	—
5·40	WILLESDEN JUNCTION	10	10 37	—
8·05	Wembley . . .	—	13 22	59
11·40	Harrow . . .	—	16 54	55
17·45	WATFORD JUNCTION	23	23 10	62½
20·95	Kings Langley . .	—	26 35	61
24·50	Hemel Hempstead .	—	30 05	60
			p.w.s.	*15
27·95	Berkhamsted . .	—	36 15	—
31·65	Tring . . .	38	41 59	—
36·10	Cheddington . .	—	45 49	79
40·20	Leighton . . .	—	48 50	85/80½
46·65	BLETCHLEY . .	51	53 33	83½/79
52·40	Wolverton . .	—	57 46	85
54·75	Castlethorpe . .	—	59 31	—
59·90	Roade . . .	63	63 33	72½
62·85	Blisworth . . .	66	65 55	76½
69·70	Weedon . . .	—	71 12	79
75·30	Welton . . .	—	75 36	70½
80·30	*Hillmorton* . .	—	79 45	75
82·55	RUGBY . . .	87	83 14	—

*Speed restriction.

Table 2
LMSR Lancaster–Penrith
Engine: 4-6-2 No. 6209 *Princess Beatrice*
Load: 14 coaches, 448 tons tare, 470 tons gross

Dist miles		*Sched* min	*Actual* min sec	*Speeds* mph
0·00	LANCASTER . .	0	0 00	—
3·10	Hest Bank . .	—	4 50	—
6·25	CARNFORTH . .	8	7 39	70½
10·75	*Burton* . . .	—	11 53	60
13·55	Milnthorpe . .	—	14 17	70½
15·45	*Hincaster Junction* .	—	16 04	59
19·10	OXENHOLME . .	21	19 50	53½
22·60	*Hay Fell* . . .	—	24 04	45½
26·15	*Grayrigg* . . .	—	29 02	40½
32·10	TEBAY . . .	36	34 48	71½
35·10	*Scout Green* . .	—	38 18	39½
37·55	*Shap Summit* . .	45	43 10	27
39·70	Shap . . .	—	45 51	—
47·00	*Clifton* . . .	—	52 17	76½
51·25	PENRITH . . .	59	56 24	—

Keeping No 6201 at work

By Michael Harris

Perhaps the trouble is that they have made it all look so easy. The scene is Sellafield station on 8 July 1980. LNER 'A4' Pacific No 4498 *Sir Nigel Gresley,* privately owned by the A4 Locomotive Society Ltd, has just worked a timetabled BR train, the 'Cumbrian Coast Express', from Carnforth. It is now ready to depart for Carlisle, preparatory to working the 'Cumbrian Mountain Express' two days later. Meanwhile, from round the curve north of the station Stanier's 'Princess Royal' No 6201 *Princess Elizabeth,* for once looking surprisingly small, comes into view running light engine from Carlisle after making an appearance at a BR open day there. No 6201 sets off with its 12-bogie train for Carnforth. All goes well and the passengers are delighted. At Steamtown, Carnforth the fire is dropped and the engine is left neat and tidy.

Just one day short, 17 years earlier, a real band of pioneers had handed over a cheque for the balance of £2,160, to complete the purchase from British Railways of *Princess Elizabeth.* What the locomotive might be doing in 1980 was probably never given a second thought at the time. It was a happy coincidence that, 17 years after the purchase of No 6201, the former Supplies & Contracts Manager of the London Midland Region, Mr

A. B. MacLeod, the official involved at the time of sale, was able to ride on the locomotive for part of its trip with a northbound 'Cumbrian Coast Express'; working.

But in 1963, the group of people who came to form The Princess Elizabeth Locomotive Society were taking a path into the unknown. Earlier that year Alan Pegler had bought *Flying Scotsman* with a view to using it for main line running. But no band of amateurs had ever saved a locomotive of the size of the 'Princess'. One of BR's conditions of sale was that a suitable site for preservation should be found. That was before today's wide range of restored railways, and a home was located at Ashchurch where the Dowty Railway Preservation Society was being formed. Withdrawn from service in October 1962, after purchase *Princess Elizabeth* worked in steam from Carlisle Kingmoor to Birmingham via the Settle & Carlisle and the Midland lines, on 12 August 1963, to be towed onwards to Ashchurch for an open day. Seventeen years later No 6201 stormed over Ais Gill with a 12 coach passenger train, in contrast to the rather surreptitious locomotive movement of 1963. The next few years after 1963 were part of the 'learning curve' of privately-owned main line steam. The hard slog of regular maintenance requirements was part of that progress; by Whit Sunday 1965 the locomotive had been steamed for the first time by its new owners.

Gradually, persistence by the Association of Railway Preservation Societies' Return to Steam Committee saw an unbending of BR's rigid attitude towards main line steam. Even before BR ran its last steam train in 1968 *Princess Elizabeth* had graced several open days at BR depots and was later one of the few locomotives to get out on BR metals during the ban on steam. It continued to do so until 1972 when it was clear that the locomotive had to be retubed, including replacement of the superheater flue tubes. This major task, the first retubing of a main line express locomotive by a preservation group on its own, began at the end of 1972, cost around £5,000 in materials, and was completed just in time for No 6201 to take its bow in the Rail 150 Calvalcade at Shildon, on 31 August 1975; the final tests to satisfy the insurers taking place 24hrs before the movement northwards.

In April 1976 the 'Princess' moved home from Ashchurch to Bulmer Railway Centre, Hereford. In view of its obvious capability the Society applied for No 6201 to be added to the list of elite locomotives accepted by BR for main line running. This is no formality, of course, and the Society's funds were further strained to cover the cost of No 6201's movement in steam to BREL Swindon Works for weighing and for ultrasonic tests on its axles; there was little change out of £1,000 for this exercise. The planned debut on the main line was the society's 'Stanier Centenary Express' of 5 June, but in the

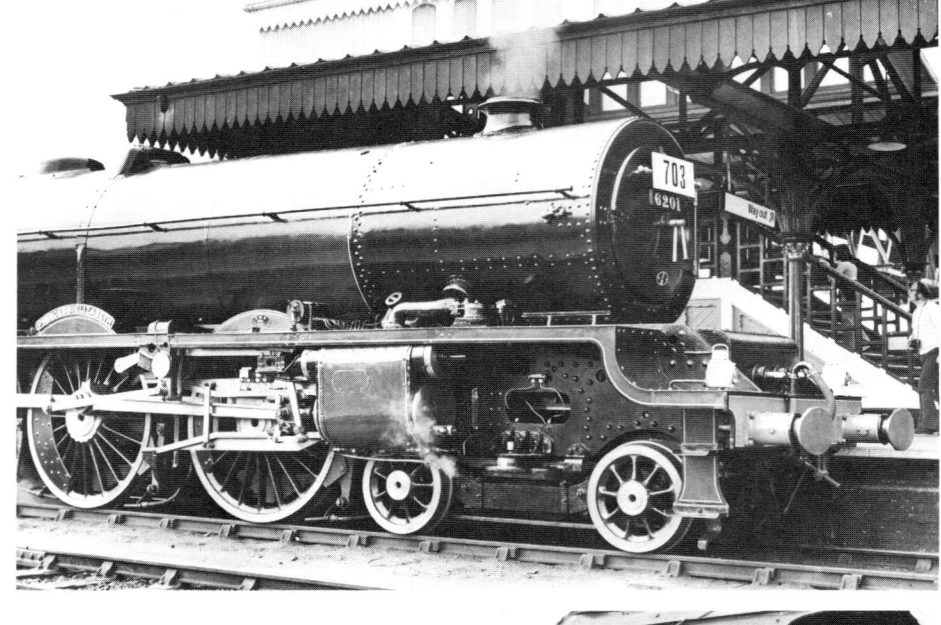

Above:
'Princess Elizabeth' hauling its first passenger train for 14 years, when deputising for *King George V* on 24 April 1976. *R.O. Coffin*

Right:
Front end detail on No 6201 taken before the Stanier centenary 703 special departed from Hereford 5 June 1976. *Peter J.C. Skelton*

Below right:
No 6201 at Hereford showing boiler drillings ready for the fitting of the 1,224 new steel stays 27 July 1979. All work being undertaken without the luxury of covered accommodation until April 1984.
G. Allen/6201 PELS

event No 6201 was called on to deputise for *King George V* on a charter train at the end of April, the 'King' having failed its hydraulic test. For all this hard work the Society was deservedly awarded the ARPS annual award for an outstanding contribution to railway preservation in 1976. More main line running followed, but in September 1978 the locomotive was stopped for a major overhaul, including complete restaying of the firebox. This was a courageous decision as it was taken to ensure that No 6201 would be able to make its appearance in the Rocket 150 Cavalcade at Rainhill in May 1980. Of course, it duly did so and subsequently it has made a triumphant return to main line running, of which more later.

What, or rather who, keeps No 6201 at work? The Society has a membership of 80 people, with a hard core of 20 members, and a working party of six. But members' subscriptions, valued though they are, would not pay to keep No 6201 on the main line. Once a main line locomotive is stopped for repairs, it is difficult to maintain support for the Society: that was especially noticeable between 1972–75. The source of funds is primarily by way of taking a sales stand to raise cash at open days, at BR depots and works and at Bulmer Railway Centre. This involves a devoted few, led by sales supremo

Tony Harries, travelling the length and breadth of the country – Nuneaton, Carlisle, Horwich, Knottingley, Derby and Hereford being just a few of the sales events attended in any year. Prize draws and the like extend the ingenuity of the Society's officials to raise cash for not only maintenance, but running costs, coal, water and oil. Whatever some may think, main line running is not self-financing, and the increasing list of funds to save locomotives from Barry provides stiff competition for the men and women trying to keep a proven main line performer in peak condition to satisfy BR's understandably tough standards for privately-owned steam.

As elsewhere, the officials of the Locomotive 6201 Princess Elizabeth Society Ltd (its full title) have changed over the years, a heartening sign that new people continue to be drawn into locomotive preservation. In charge of things there is Chairman Ken Andrews, Secretary Clive Mojonnier and Engineer Eric Ellis, in charge of the working party.

Eric is by training a ships' engineer, basically versed in triple expansion engines, but attracted to No 6201 primarily because of its engineering, more than as a railway enthusiast. His Norfolk & Western RR engineer's hat and No 6201's additional Canadian chime whistle betray Engineer Ellis's admiration of North American steam. After the 'Princess' was stopped in September 1978, Eric and three others each spent 100 'spare' days on the back-breaking job of overhaul work. Except for Christmas Day and Boxing Day Eric spent the Christmas holiday week making stays. In addition, all

Right:
1980 once again saw a 'Lizzie' working out of Liverpool, one of its old haunts. This was to be on a special train after No 6201's appearance at Rainhill.
J.H. Cooper-Smith

Below:
Lord and Princess meet. Nos 850 and 6201 at Carnforth on 10 July where she was based ready to haul the September 'Cumbrian Coast Express'. *J.H. Cooper-Smith*

Left:
Crossing, Esk Meals viaduct on the return 'Lancastrian' to Carnforth 25 August 1980. *John S. Whiteley*

Below left:
Under the coaling tower at Carnforth prior to hauling the 'Cumbrian Coast Express' of 2 September 1980. *W. A. Sharman*

concerned worked hard at sales events, for without these and draws, donations, and receipts from main line running, the £2,500 cost of restaying the firebox could not be financed.

In all, 1,224 stays were replaced, the replacements all being made and fitted by the hard working team; the rest of the work involved the outside of the boiler being exposed, de-rusted, relagged and repainted; the eccentrics remetalled and remachined; the lubricating system renovated and cab fittings overhauled. The Society's Brian Lancaster deserves particular commendation for making a fine job of repainting, lining out and relettering the locomotive; not forgetting that this was preceded by derusting and surface preparation. If all this seems hard graft, then don't forget the equal effort of keeping the locomotive in traffic: routine maintenance, oiling up, coaling and keeping a careful eye on water samples. The locomotive may well satisfy its main appetite with Daw Mill Colliery (Whitacre) coal, but time, money and effort are swallowed metaphorically speaking at much the same rate. However, the Society can afford to feel proud of *Princess Elizabeth,* and the BR running inspectors covering the trips from Carnforth have made no secret that they consider the locomotive is in fine fettle.

Unhappily, its 1980 return to main line running was affected by the fire risk ban on steam movements for its first scheduled charter train of 17 May. After Rainhill, and a trip with a Steam One-Five-O Manchester–Liverpool special, the locomotive moved to Steamtown, Carnforth, a temporary base for the summer. From there it worked the 'Cumbrian Coast Express' south on 8 July, north on 2 September; the 'Cumbrian Mountain Express' on 4 September; the 'Lancastrian No 2' charter train on 25 August, and returned to Hereford with the Society's 'Red Rose' charter train of 27 September, heading it through from Carnforth to Chester via Hellifield, Manchester Vic, Northwich and Chester. For the 1980/81 winter season No 6201 was scheduled to work the 'Welsh Marches Express' on various occasions. Obviously No 6201's absence from the main line between 1978–80 was enforced, but the Society is also concerned that the engine shouldn't become over-exposed in terms of the public appearances it makes. This seems sensible as it ensures continued support for the regular steam workings, such as those based on Carnforth, if some of the booked locomotives have a rarity value.

It might seem silly to ask what drives people to devote so much of their spare time away from home, in often far from ideal working conditions, tackling difficult engineering tasks, or cheerfully carrying out the jobs of a manual labourer in preparing

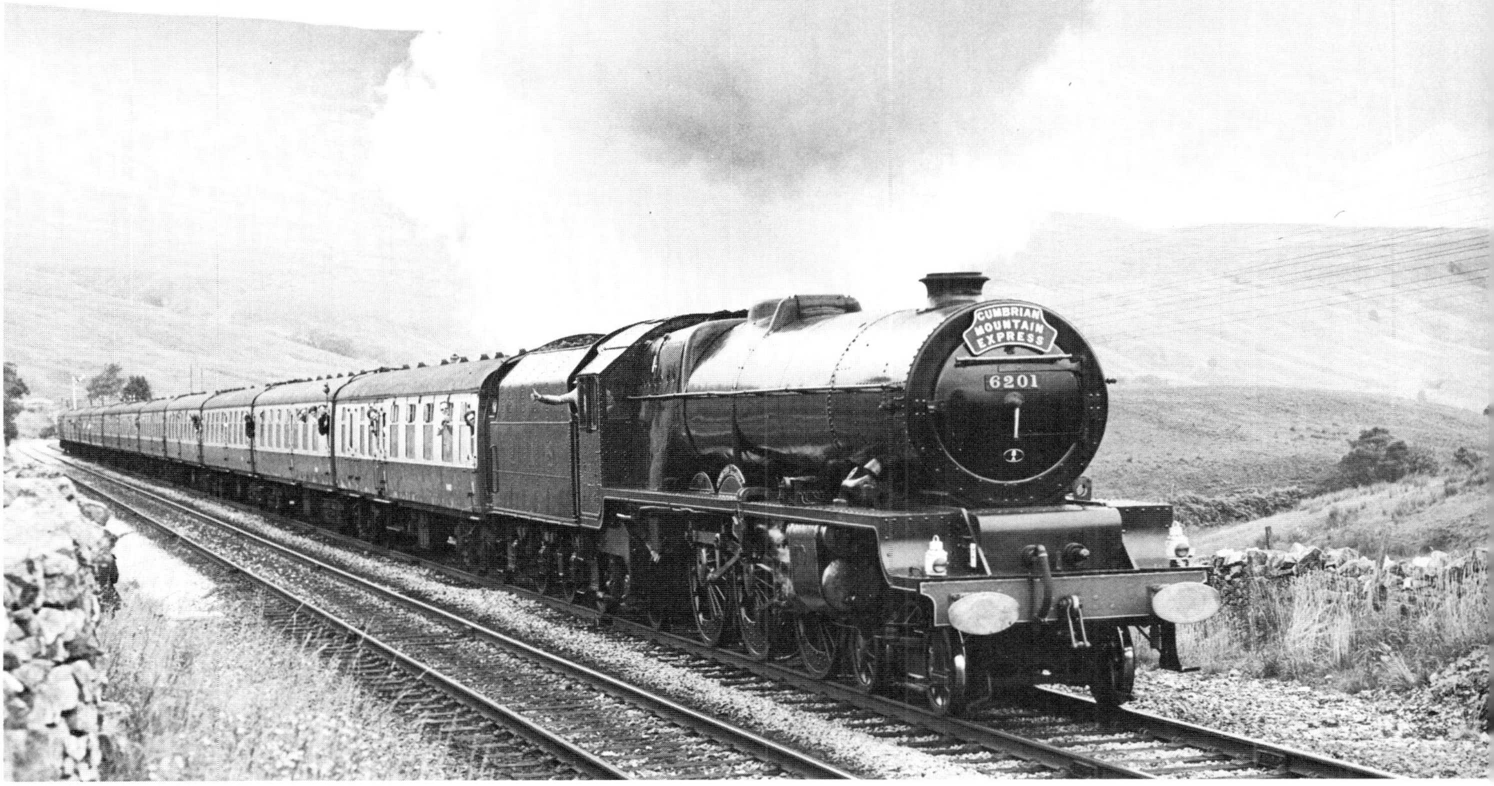

Above:
No 6201 at Ais Gill achieving exceptional timings on this section hauling the 'Cumbrian Mountain Express' 4 September 1980.
G.W. Morrison

the locomotive. When Eric Ellis, the Society's Engineer, said that it was because the engineering of the locomotive inpressed him, and that it satisfied his thirst for knowledge, that seemed a reasonable explanation, but not one necessarily applicable to other people. But second thoughts suggested that these reasons were the basis of most people's love of the steam locomotive. The appeal of its engineering with its essential simplicity and solidity are at the heart of things, and however much one reads and learns about the steam locomotive, there is still more to find out.

As we have seen, without a vigorous sales activity the 'Princess' would not be available for main line service. Certainly, even with a heavy programme of charter trains and BR services, the costs of routine maintenance and repairs would not be covered by the receipts alone. Three points made an impression on your writer. First, that only in 1980 had the society managed to pay off the last loan for the work incurred in the 1972–75 retubing. Second, it was to hear a 'Cumbrian Mountain Express' patron surmise that presumably the fee the society received for BR's hire of No 6201 covered depreciation; the word is unknown and probably meaningless for main steam locomotives today and if it could be assessed would make steam working prohibitively expensive. Third, there was the news that over in Canada the

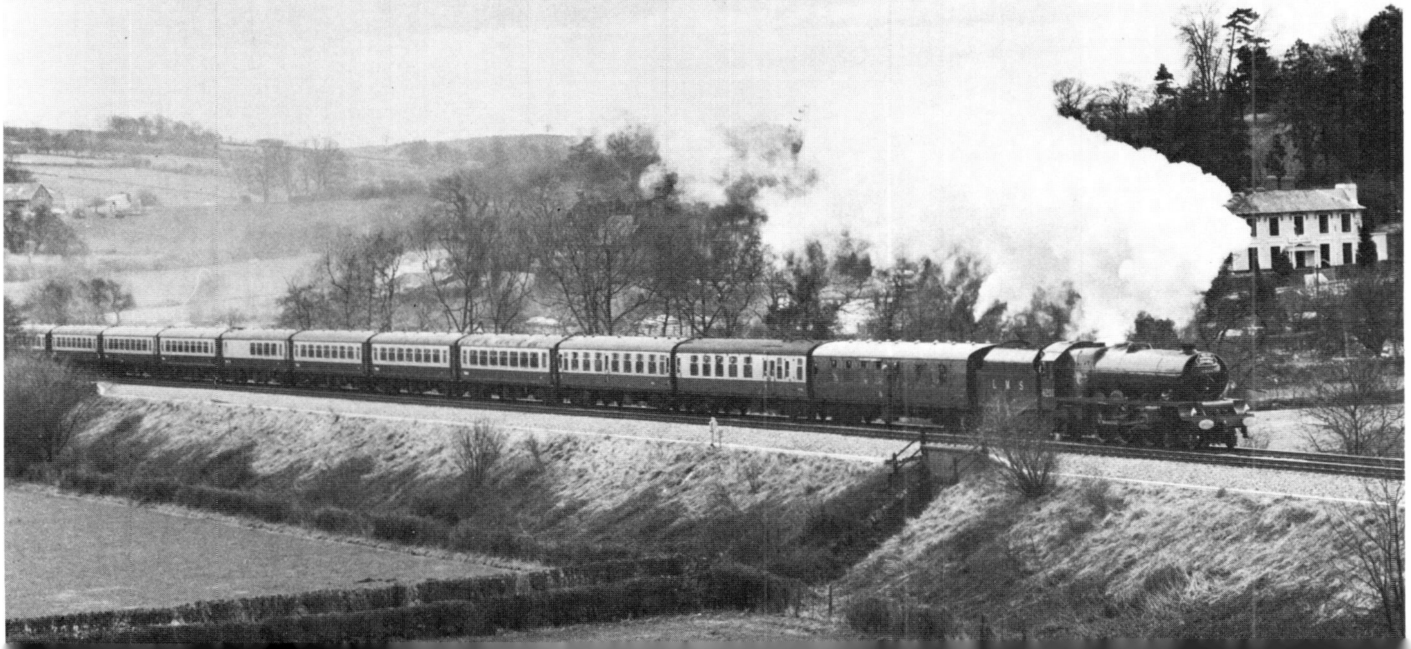

Below:
on the 'Welsh Marches Pullman' turn No 6201 climbs towards Llanvihangel bank at Pandy from Hereford to Newport 30 January 1982 the day that slipping occurred. *W.A. Sharman*

bulletnose Canadian National No 6060 was to finish main line running because its boiler needed retubing. This would have to be done professionally but there was no suggestion that a group of professional amateurs might do the job. There is no greater credit to people such as the working party of the Locomotive 6201 Princess Elizabeth Society Ltd that a national railway system should accept their work as meeting professional standards.

The writer was lucky to ride behind No 6201. The first occasion was with the 'Cumbrian Coast Express' on 8 July. Although no fireworks were called for with the 12-coach train, it was a competent performance, made memorable by the majestic four-cylinder beat of the locomotive as it was put to work. A short footplate ride from Grange-over-Sands to Carnforth found the BR inspector and crew enthusiastic and complimentary about No 6201. A better clue to the prowess of the locomotive came with the 'Cumbrian Mountain Express' on 4 September, working south from Carlisle to Skipton with 12 coaches of 423 tons tare, 450 tons gross. The section to Appleby produced some satisfying bursts of throaty 'stack noise' but the real interest was on the climb to Ais Gill. The initial 1 in 100 from Ormside–Griseburn saw speed at 39/40mph, then 51/52mph on the easier section past Crosby Garrett.

Beyond Kirby Stephen a steady 46mph was attained on the 1 in 100, with 47/48 past Mallerstang and 45mph on most of the final ascent to Ais Gill, with an absolute minimum of 43. This took us past the summit box, 17.55 miles from Appleby, in 25min 10sec. The nine-coach 'Waverley' express from Edinburgh–St Pancras in the late 1950s was allowed 24min start to pass on this section, so with a train over 100ton heavier No 6201 had done extremely well. The engine was worked at between 25–30% cut off and full regulator and the crew consisted of Messrs E. Doubtfire, P. McDermot and J. Brown of Skipton, with Preston's Inspector Cullen in attendance. Reference to the series of controlled road test results over the Settle and Carlisle in the 1950s will show how fine the achievement of men and machine was in these preservation days.

In January 1982 a further trip behind No 6201 was made on a 'Welsh Marches Pullman' turn. When leaving Abergavenny from a standing position the conditions are worth noting. Locomotive and train had just performed a run past for the passengers. From the cab the climb to Llanvihangel is visible immediately while waiting in the platform. With rain and diesel oil on the track, and 500 tons behind the locomotive, these are ideal conditions for a slip. And yet some members of the public were surprised at the bout of uncontrolled slipping that took place.

With most Pacific types of locomotive, they are notably light-footed and if water carries over into the cylinders this creates a hydraulic effect.

Originally when the 'Princess Royal' class was built it was rumoured that William Stanier was going to fit one of the locomotives with equalised suspension driving wheels, which may have aided starting.

So today we see the society continuing to preserve an example of Sir William Stanier's work. Under extreme conditions over 23 years of ownership, the society at last has cover for the locomotive. This came in the shape of an engine shed finished in April 1984, contributed to not only by 6201 members, but 6000 Locomotive Association, Merchant Navy Locomotive Preservation Society and H. P. Bulmer. At long last the precious man hours lost by the vagaries of the weather can be capitalised on. This is an important step, as the society now face the second retubing of the locomotive, in its care. Not only finance will be required, but man hours provided in holidays and days off, to ensure the locomotive once again graces the main line.

Below:
No 6201 finally under cover, after 23 years, in its new shed at the Bulmer Railway Centre.
Peter J. C. Skelton

Society Fireman

The scene is not so unusual for the 1980s. There is a crowd at least four or five deep at the end of Shrewsbury station, all waiting apparently aimlessly on this bright Saturday morning, even if it is rather cold for the time of year. A hoot in the distance and the whole panoply of advanced technology from Nikon, Canon, Kodak and Agfa is brought to bear on the monster as it rounds the triangle outside the station. On this occasion it is a steam locomotive and coach only and there is a sudden surge from the crowd as everyone strives for a better view as the Pacific turns on the triangle around the large signalbox. There is little thought perhaps for the people aboard that locomotive and coach and, in particular, the man who has prepared the engine for the road. In today's circumstances, that task is usually split between two people – the engineer and the fireman who 'lights-up'.

The engineer will have got the locomotive ready a day or so before the rail tour, by oiling the bearings, lubrication points and axleboxes and giving the locomotive a mechanical check.

The fireman's task, probably, will have started on the Thursday evening previous to Saturday's 'WME' when he will have packed his overalls, boots, food and kit ready for the trip to the loco shed the first thing on the Friday morning. Then he is off to an early bed to store up as much sleep as possible.

As fireman, I have to be awake at 05.00 on the Friday to catch the 07.30 train for Hereford, arriving there at about 11.30, to collect milk, bread, and keys. The shed is reached at 12.30, just in time for lunch.

Once refreshed, the task starts in earnest. Firewood must be collected, tools packed on the back of the tender (spanners, crowbars, oil, water treatment, rope, hosepipes, paraffin, nuts and bolts, two shovels, coal-pick, hand-brushes, bucket and the inevitable box of spare corks for the oil seals which are often removed from the engine by our admirers for souvenirs) and lamps to be filled – two front lamps, one rear and one for the water gauge glasses in the cab.

Before the fire can be laid, let alone lit, a complete check of both locomotive and tender has to be carried out. In order, this comprises: Front End – to ensure that the chimney is unobstructed, the front end of the tubeplate is free from leakage, that all blanking/washout plugs are tight, that the smokebox is clean and free of char from the last trip, that the blastpipe is unobstructed and to check that the smokebox door is tightly fastened so as to retain the smokebox vacuum when running. Next the Rear End – see that the ashpan and grate are cleaned out, that the three lead safety plugs are secure in the top of the firebox roof, that the rear tubeplate is clear with no leaks, that all firebox stays and riveted seams are tight and dry and that the brick arch in the firebox is free of cracks. The gauges (water, pressure, vacuum, speed, carriage heating) and whistle will have been fitted by the Engineer and the boiler filled with water. About 10/11 tons of best Daw Mill cobbles will be loaded in the tender, along with 4,000 gallons (18 tons) of water and some water treatment for the boiler.

As to the boiler, the main thing remaining is to see that all the plugs and mudhole doors are locked in position and not leaking. Even the slightest weep when cold may be a major catastrophe once there is steam at 250lb/sq in pressure in the boiler.

The above process of checking, loading and preparation will have taken two to three hours. The Society has a training programme for those members learning to be firemen and being schooled to pass the test required by the Motive Power Inspectorate. This is so that they can work on their own as firemen in due course. With a trainee present, as much as double the normal time is required to prepare the engine.

The fire can now be laid, with the dampers opened, in similar style to a domestic fire, but on a much larger scale as the grate is about 6ft wide and 7ft long. First paper, then old oily rags, wood and, finally, small pieces of coal about the size of a man's fist. This should give a pile about 2ft high and 4–5ft in diameter. The protector and smoke deflector plates are then placed in the firehole of the boiler. The fire is normally lit about 12 hours before the locomotive is required to leave the site. This may seem a long time, and certainly is by some standards, but by doing it this way sudden stressing of the boiler is avoided, thereby reducing maintenance in the long-term and prolonging active life.

But there are two things that must be done before lighting-up – to check that there is water in the boiler and in the tender, too.

The moment of decision has arrived and

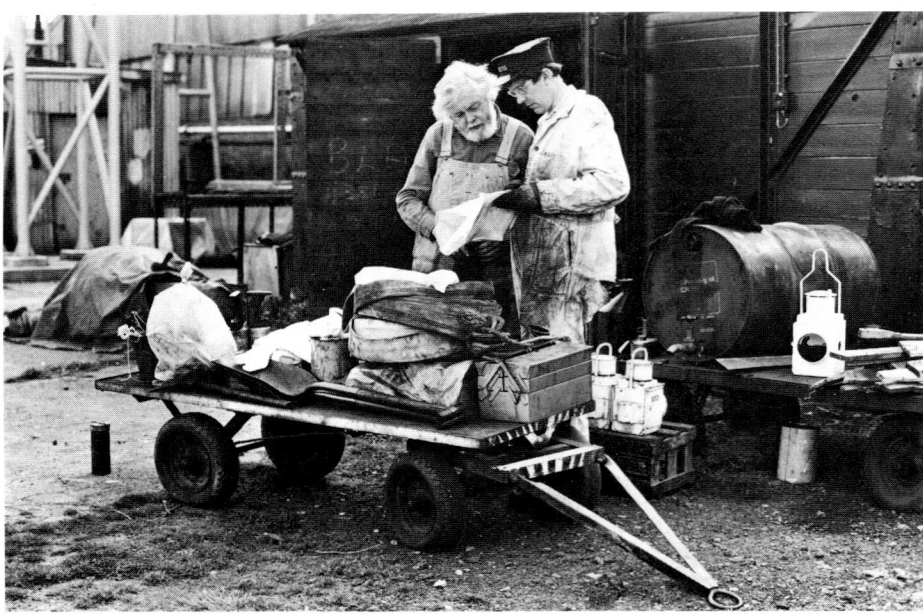

two firelighters are placed on the shovel, lit and placed in a hole made in the pile of wood and coal on the grate. This may seem a simple operation, but there is a snag. The last place the smoke goes on a 'Princess Royal' is up the chimney and so the cab is filled with thick, sulphurous smoke and fumes which make life almost impossible. Depending on the prevailing wind, this situation might continue for the next four hours or so until steam is being produced which will draw the smoke away from the fire. The fire needs making up about every 45min, a process which inevitably results in sore eyes, burnt hands and black faces for the uninitiated. As the boiler expands with the heat being produced, it eases backwards with grinding noises until stabilising after 4–5 hours.

At about midnight on Friday/Saturday, other colleagues have gone to bed after helping to clean the engine and tender. The fireman now feels free to have a sit-down and to rest for a while, even, perhaps, to fit in a cooked meal and a short nap between the continuing rounds of firing every hour. During the day, its been a case of snatching tea or snacks when possible – or not at all. With a bit of luck, the night will be dry and warm with a slight breeze. If not, it will be cold, wet and miserable – just to help matters along.

05.00 on Saturday and the fireman wakes his sleeping colleagues with a mug of tea so that they can wash and breakfast before the final cleaning of the locomotive and tender. Coal supplies must be topped up (just over a ton has been used in lighting-up and raising steam) and water taken if required. Then comes the job of securing the nameplates and builders' plates (someone is bound to ask during the day why the nameplates aren't left on the engine all the time) and the train headboard is secured to the top of the smokebox, the head lamps are lit and tail lamp attached to the Society's coach which will accompany No 6201 on its trip.

Before the British Rail crew arrive, the injectors that feed cold water into the boiler are operated to check that they are functioning correctly. By now, the boiler pressure is showing about 200lb/sq in, the maximum pressure being 250lb/sq in. The footplate is swept and washed clean of any coal, ash and debris, ready for the BR driver to take the locomotive and to collect the coach from the other end of the shed yard.

With a bit of luck the fireman can now have a wash, get into clean overalls, have some breakfast and take his well-deserved place in the coach behind the engine on the 51-mile journey to Shrewsbury from Hereford. For the first time in 26 hours there is a chance to get some sleep, only to be roused at Shrewsbury where water is taken and the coal pushed forward in the tender ready for the remainder of the trip.

The rest of the day's outing just becomes a blur: more Nikons, Rolleis, Instamatics, and the rest. Why don't you do 'this', 'that', or the 'other'? 'We want to see more of the

Above:
Princess Elizabeth near Ponthir working a 'Welsh Marches Express' from Newport 25 April 1981. *Peter J.C. Skelton*

Right:
No 6201 passes Wooferton with the 'Midland Jubilee' special of 1 October 1977. This celebrated Queen Elizabeth II's silver jubilee, 6201 representing the LMS of the four old companies. *Peter J.C. Skelton*

Below:
The fireman on the right, schooling his trainee before a main line run. *Peter J.C. Skelton*

engine!' 'How do you steer it?' 'Does it burn oil?' 'Do Butlins pay for it?' 'Where's the accelerator?' 'Did you get it from Barry?' And so on and on and on!

With the run over and the engine back on shed, the job is far from finished. The BR crew of driver, fireman and footplate inspector will be booking off duty, but the locomotive has to be put to bed. The fire is

raked and shovelled out (a very hot and arduous task, ideal for removing skin from knuckles and for burning fingers and hands), the boiler filled and the ashpan cleaned if the engine is required again within the next few days. As this is taking place the engineer will be checking around the engine, as indeed he has done at stops during the day, to see that nothing has broken, or fallen off. All tools are packed away again and the nameplates, shovels and lamps returned to store ready for the next time the engine goes main line.

At last, after nearly 40 hours I am home again with only one thought in mind – to sleep the next day through – then, back to work on Monday. So after one day's holiday and the weekend gone, was it worth it?

The trip with the 'WME' mentioned above is not one of the longer ones. The August 1980 'Red Rose' involved us in travelling from Birmingham, to Hereford, Crewe and Carnforth and then with the engine from Carnforth to Manchester, Chester, Shrewsbury and Hereford. This was no joke, and a journey never to be forgotten. So was the one when some of us working on the locomotive returned 'on the cushions' to Hereford in a train full of football hooligans. This lot turned a first class coach into two sets of bogies and a steel shell, without windows, fittings or seating in no time at all.

So if you are one of those on the lineside or station platform end, please give a thought to the men who have helped to get the locomotive ready, whatever the weather, for the public to admire, savour and photograph.

See you all again soon – I think!

Top left:
No 4930 *Hagley Hall* alongside No 6201 being prepared at the Bulmer Railway Centre for hauling the 'Welsh Marches Pullman' on 30 January 1982. *Peter J. C. Skelton*

Centre:
With no banker No 6201 tops Miles Platting bank, with the 'Red Rose; of 27 September 1980 on its way back to Hereford. Similar to the events of 1936 on arrival at Hereford No 6201 was found to have lost white metal from a cross head. *J.H. Cooper-Smith*

Left:
This could easily have been a photograph of No 6201 in its early years. Seen on 27 September 1980 passing Burnden junction, Bolton, the longest trip the firemen had experienced with No 6201 Carnforth–Hereford. *A. Oldfield*

Top right:
No 6201 hauling the 'Cumbrian Coast Express' passing Whitbeck, Cumbria, on 2 September 1980. *Paul Claxton*

Centre right:
A study in speed – No 6201 in preservation days at Ponthir 30 January 1982. *Peter J.C. Skelton*

Right:
'Lizzie's' last main line duty in 1982 on 20 March before withdrawal for tender repairs. Seen here bursting from under a stone road bridge after emerging from the southern exit of Dinmore tunnel. *Peter J.C. Skelton*

Milestones in the Society's History

1961
October — Fund started to preserve 6201 *Princess Elizabeth*.
1962
20 October — 6201 withdrawn as 'outside authorised programme.
1963 — 6201 bought from British Rail for £2,160, 75% cheque written 11 February 1963 and the balance 9 July 1963.
7 August — Nameplates collected from Crewe Works stores.
12 August — 6201 left Carlisle (Kingmoor) for Birmingham via Leeds & Ais Gill.
31 August — Engine arrived at Ashchurch from Birmingham (towed). Society formed.
1965 — Sales team started.
Whit Sunday — Trial steaming of 6201 at Ashchurch – result OK.
1966 — Members decide to change livery to 1936 style of crimson-lake.
1967
21 October — First visit to BR open day at Bristol (Bath Road).
1968
Spring — Boiler cladding of locomotive still being de-rusted.
1969
January — LMS Type Stove 'R' arrives at Ashchurch.
28 September — Tyseley open day.
1970
May — Final lettering & lining out of engine completed.
1972
1 October — Engine at Tyseley open day with LMS 5428 on shuttle service.
1973
1 July — First old small tube out of boiler of 6201, last out November.
1974
February — Boiler exam by Eagle Star – requested 5 flue tubes to be removed.
May — Commence to remove flue tubes in total after condemning.
June — All flue tubes removed.
October — Boiler being prepared for new tubes.
1975
April — Flue tubes delivered on site.
21 July — Boil out of boiler after retubing.
26 July — British Rail steam test– members steaming at Ashchurch.
28 July — Leave Ashchurch for Shildon at 00.50, 06.01 Chesterfield, 08.42 York station platform 14, then Stockton and Shildon.
31 August — Shildon Cavalcade, exhibit 23, started at 14.00.
1 September — To Ashchurch with 35028 *Clan Line* and four coaches via Darlington Bank Top shed yard left at 23.30 on 31 August 1975 then Sheffield for water, Derby at 09.00.
1976
3 February — Limited company formed.
February–June — Re-metalled both outside crossheads & connecting rod big ends, eight steel firebox stays replaced.
5 April — British Rail steam test, at Ashchurch.
6 April — Leave Ashchurch for Swindon BREL Works, depart 08.00 and arrive at 12.00 via Eckington, Chipping Sodbury, Parkway and Stoke Gifford Triangle. Work carried out – weighing and ultrasonic testing of axles.
10 April — Leave Swindon BREL Works for BRC Hereford, via Didcot for turning, Filton, Glos, Severn Tunnel Jnc, Newport, Hereford. This was a 15 hour journey – we crossed River Wye at 17.15.
24 April — First main line tour – deputised for *King George V* on Hereford, Shrewsbury, Newport, Hereford 'Gwentman' and 'Inter City' tours.
1 June — British Rail steam test.
5 June — First society rail tour – the Sir W.A. Stanier Centenary Special train departed from platform 8 Euston, 6201 wore '703' headboard and Mr R.A. Riddles was guest of honour and rode on the footplate wearing a white coat as on the record run in 1936. Engine 6201 worked train from Hereford to Chester and back.

2 October	Charter special, Hereford–Shrewsbury–Hereford with 468 tons.
October	Replacement of 40 steel stays in firebox sides.

1977

12 January	Stove 'R' coach arrived at Hereford from Ashchurch by rail.
29 January	The ARPS Award presented to Society at York.
23 April	Charter special, Hereford–Chester–Hereford with *KGV* 'Cathedrals Express'.
24 September	6201 Society members steaming day – it rained!
1/8 October	SLOA 'Silver Jubilee' specials, Hereford to Craven Arms then Shrewsbury light engine for water then Craven Arms LE to pick up train for return to Hereford. NCB made film of tour.

1978

20 May	Charter special, MLST and Southern Homes, Hereford–Chester and return.
15 July	In steam at Hereford for the Branch Line Society.
23/4 September	In steam Hereford open day for last time prior to re-staying.
20 November	10 year boiler exam by Eagle Star – verdict 'Fit'.
17 December	Work started to strip off old nuts off the stays.

1979

January	Invited to attend 'Rocket 150' at Rainhill.
4 March	All stay nuts off.
22 April	First old stay knocked out.
August	Steel delivered for manufacture of new stays.

1980

3 February	The last of the old stays out.
17 February	All new stays in.
6 March	Hydraulic test passed, British Rail and Eagle Star.
9 March	All new stay nuts on.
29 April	Engine fired for boil out, assembly now complete.
9 May	BR steam test passed, engine and tender repainted.
17 May	SLOA steam special, 'Lancastrian' from Chester to Manchester (Victoria), day of the fire hazard and 6201 went in light steam only from Chester hauled by diesel 47.182 – 6201 then on to Bold Colliery to be the first engine on site, arrived on time at 14.55.
24/5/6/ May	Participation in the 'Rocket 150' cavalcade at Rainhill, weather indifferent – cold but sunny on the Saturday and rain on the Monday. American chime whistle on the loco on the Monday, 26 May in order to out 'hoot' 4498 *Sir Nigel Gresley,* worked well.
27 May–7 June	Engine on exhibition at CEGB Power Station, Bold following Rainhill.
10 June	Movement of engine to Manchester (Liverpool Road) coupled to Nos 4472 *Flying Scotsman,* 26020, two BSKs, coach GE1 and a goods brake van. Left Bold at 10.20 for Liverpool to turn and then back to Manchester. 6201 was the first locomotive into the old station. In the process of being steamed into the covered shed 6201 became derailed, (front bogie), Newton Heath BR breakdown team eventually arrived to lift 6201 back on to the track.
25 June	An '08' class diesel shunter moved the engine to Newton Heath MPD for a mechanical examination to check on any damage that may have been caused by the derailment. It passed OK.
29 June	British Rail 'Rocket One-Five-O' special from Manchester to Liverpool Edge Hill calling at Earlestown and Rainhill, train incorrectly marshalled as 6000LA BSK then 11 BR coaches and FSE GE1 inadvertantly coupled on for a free ride! On the way back a stone thrown through cab window firemans side front, stone hit footplate Inspector and 6201 member.
30 June	Positional move from Manchester Liverpool Road, (start 09.45), to Carnforth Steamtown, (arrive 14.00) via Bolton (10.57) Blackburn for water, (11.15–11.45), and Hellifield, (12.30–13.00).
4 July	Positional move, Carnforth – Skipton – Carlisle Upperby Depot where we arrived at 13.50. 17 years almost to the day when the loco was last in Carlisle.
5/6 July	Open Days Carlisle Upperby MPD, 6201 wears a 12B shedplate in honour of the occasion. Engine accompanied by replica of *Rocket* driven by John Bellwood, Engineer of NRM.
8 July	Positional move light engine from Carlisle to Sellafield, the first Stanier Pacific over this route? Hauled Cumbrian Coast Express back to Carnforth.
12 August	Hauled British Rail train, Cumbrian Coast Express from Sellafield to Carnforth after working light engine from Carnforth to Sellafield in the morning.
13 August	Worked the Steamtown, Carnforth shuttle.
14 August	Light engine movement to Skipton then hauled British Rail train 'Cumbrian Mountain Express' from Skipton back to Carnforth.
25 August	Light engine movement from Carnforth – Sellafield, then hauled SLOA Charter special 'Lancastrian 2' railtour from Sellafield to Carnforth.

2 September	Worked British Rail train 'Cumbrian Coast Express' from Carnforth to Sellafield then light engine to Carlisle via the Maryport and Carlisle line. Stabled at Upperby Depot.
3 September	6201 stands at Carlisle Upperby MPD.
4 September	Hauled British Rail train 'Cumbrian Mountain Express' from Carlisle to Skipton, record run up the bank to Ais Gill Summit from Appleby in 25 minutes with 12 coaches.
27 September	The Society organised special train the 'Red Rose' from Crewe to Carnforth hauled by the last electric locomotive of Class 84 in service, arrived 60min late! 6201 then hauled the train from Carnforth to Chester via Blackburn, Manchester Victoria and up the bank without assistance to Miles Platting onto Northwich, at Mickle Trafford 6201 was held at a signal and the Driver could not restart her despite many heavy slips. Aid summoned from Chester, Carriage & Wagon staff diagnosed the fault in the coaching stock with the brakes of the last vehicle being hard on. 6201 and train piloted by a Class 47 diesel to Chester where steam section was terminated and special ran back to Crewe. *Princess Elizabeth* returned to Hereford via Shrewsbury without stopping for water at Crewe Bank.
Winter	Ashpan repaired with temporary patch, new blower pipe fitted and two small tubes removed from boiler for examination new ones then fitted.

1981

14 February	SLOA charter special, 'Welsh Marches Express' – 6201 light engine plus BSK from Hereford to Shrewsbury then hauled train back to Hereford, recovered 30min of late start from Shrewsbury!
7 March	Hauled 'Welsh Marches Express' for SLOA from Shrewsbury back to Hereford after the run north light engine with BSK.
11 April	6201 hauled the 'Welsh Marches Express' for SLOA from Hereford to Newport and return to Hereford. First run past of engine at Abergavenny.
18 April	6201 hauls the Welsh Marches Express from Shrewsbury to Hereford, oil on track just short of the top of the back to Church Stretton engine slips and goes off beat with broken valve rings.
25 April	'Welsh Marches Express' – 6201 ran from Hereford to Newport and back to Hereford, photographic 'run past' at Abergavenny.
6 August	Last remains of water scoop gear removed from under tender and stored.
Winter	Piston valves removed and reringed at Nottingham at Xmas on a kitchen table, too much snow to get to Hereford by road!

1982

2 January	All valves refitted and drive connected up. New injector pipes fitted and all cab pipework annealed.
21 January	British Rail steam test passed.
30 January	Welsh Marches Pullman, 6201 hauls 500 tons trailing from Hereford to Newport and return.
20 March	'Welsh Marches Pullman', 6201 runs from the railway centre to Shrewsbury light engine then hauls 'WMP' back to Hereford, we suffer a broken cab spectacle window from a dislodged brick from the roof of Dinmore tunnel.
6/7/8/ July	BRC Hereford, 6201 in steam at an event known as 'All our Futures' held to entertain schoolchildren.
28 September	Body of tender lifted from frames for overhaul using a 40 ton hydraulic mobile crane.
Winter	Brake gear and springs stripped ready for refurbishment, all bearings remetalled on tender. Ashpan rebuilt and damper doors made good. Engine inside motion overhauled.

1983

14 October	British Rail steam test, informed at the test by BR WR that on a seven year rule must be followed, consequently *no* 50th anniversary run for locomotive.

1984

1 April	New locomotive shed at Hereford Railway Centre is completed and 6201 is the first engine in, the loco had never been under permanent cover until now.
22/23 April	Open Day BRC Hereford and 6201 is in steam, Mrs C. Fleet rides on the footplate and sits in the firemans seat used by her husband on the record run in 1936.
December	The new set of small boiler tubes arrive at Hereford from British Steel, Corby, they are placed alongside the loco!

1985

January	Ready to begin second retubing of locomotive for a return to main line running.

6201 can be seen at the Bulmer Railway Centre, Hereford, either on static display or in steam most bank holiday weekends through the year.